Best
MOM
ROCKFORD
Erin Sturm

Reedy Press
PO Box 5131
St. Louis, MO 63139
reedypress.com

Library of Congress Control Number: 2023952185

ISBN: 9781681065014

Printed in the United States of America
24 25 26 27 28   5 4 3 2 1

Cover and title page art courtesy of Dan Zettwoch.
Images courtesy of Erin Sturm unless marked.
Line art courtesy of FreePik, Shutterstock, or believed to be in the public domain.

Dedication

To my children, Norah and Miles: every place in this book holds memories of your childhoods. Thank you for giving me a chance to see Rockford, and the world, through your eyes. You two are magic. Love you to infinity.

Table of Contents

Introduction

Raising kids in Rockford totally rocks! Rockford has music, culture, nature, science, art, and so much more! There is something for everyone in the Forest City, no matter what you and your kids are interested in.

Get outdoors and explore the 44 beautiful and scenic forest preserves in Winnebago County to connect with nature. Get active and try a new sport. Rockford offers unique sports like BMX, tubing, snowboarding, and wakeboarding for your kids to try.

Check out Rockford's nationally renowned children's museum and Japanese gardens. Feel pride in knowing Rockford has played a part in history. Spend the day visiting spots on the Rockford Peaches trail to celebrate one of the world's best women's baseball teams of all time. Take your budding paleontologists to visit the world's most well-preserved juvenile T. rex right here in Rockford.

Rockford's vibrant arts and music scene is perfect for kids of all ages to enjoy. Families can gather downtown throughout the spring, summer, and fall for a huge city market, grab dinner at a weekly food truck roundup, or welcome the holiday season at the biggest holiday party you've ever seen.

There's no limit to the amount of fun you and your kids can have while staying right here in the Forest City.

Best Place to Explore Nature's Playground

THE GROVE NATURE PLAYSCAPE

8786 Montague Rd. | 815-335-2915
seversondells.com

Imagine a playground made entirely of natural materials that blends beautifully into the peaceful landscape. You're picturing the Grove Nature Playscape located in Severson Dells Nature Center. Severson Dells is a 369-acre forest preserve with woodlands, fields, a stream and pond, dells, and dolomite cliffs. There are more than two miles of paved walkways and a nature center where educational and environmentally friendly events are regularly held.

The Grove Nature Playscape is a kid's dream! It has five unstructured play sections that are perfect for creative minds. In the sound exploration area, kids can create beautiful music on a rustic harp and drums. In the create area, they can build structures from wooden blocks and tree coins. Kids who enjoy performing can put on a show on the stage located in the center of the Grove. In the art area, colorful suncatchers allow kids to see the play space through a rainbow lens. Thrill seekers can scale leaning tree branches to check out the view from 15 feet in the air.

The Grove is open year-round and is free to the public. Bring bug spray, reef-safe sunscreen, and reusable water bottles. Make a day of it by packing a picnic lunch and enjoying it at one of the tables overlooking The Grove. The nearby nature center has bathrooms and water bottle refillers inside.

LEVINGS PARK

1420 S Pierpont Ave.
rockfordparkdistrict.org/levings-park

Two more great places to play among the trees are Levings Park playgrounds. These two newer play structures are within view of Levings Lake where West Rock Wake Park is located. The first playground is smaller with slides, musical instruments, and balancing blocks. The playground is shaded and comfortable even during the hot summer. The second playground is only a short walk from the first, and is treehouse themed with an inclusive zip line with harness, slides, and swings including a mom-and-baby swing. This park is only minutes from The Grove at Severson Dells.

How to be a best mom:

- **Pack a lunch and watch the wakeboarders while you eat!**
- **Play a game of hopscotch on the painted path.**

SINNISSIPPI PARK

1401 N 2nd St. | 815-987-8858

For more fun in a woodsy setting, Sinnissippi Park offers two playgrounds surrounded by nature's beauty. The first is designed specifically for toddlers and has a musical theme with xylophone and drums on-site. The playground is the perfect size for kids ages 1–5 to climb, slide, and spin. The second playground is geared toward kids ages 5–12 and includes a ninja-warrior-style climbing structure, swings, a spinning feature, and a 30-foot-tall double slide. The park also includes pickleball courts and a golf course for parents to play too!

How to be a best mom:

- **Bring your bikes or scooters to ride on the paved paths throughout the park.**
- **Try to spot the many fairy doors on trees throughout the park!**

Best Place to Splash Around

KLEHM ARBORETUM & BOTANIC GARDEN

2715 S Main St. | 815-965-8146
klehm.org

Splash and play the day away while being surrounded by nature's beauty! Located in the heart of Klehm Arboretum & Botanic Garden, Nancy Olson Kid's Creek is a summertime favorite. The structure was built to enhance the natural beauty of the area while giving kids a place to cool off on a hot day. The splash pad and kid's creek are nature themed with creek beds, fountains, pools, and streams for kids to play in. Kids can walk through the creek and play in the shallow pools, which are perfect for sitting down and relaxing. At the deepest, the pools are around 15 inches.

In addition to the Kid's Creek, Klehm hosts traveling exhibits in the summers that families can walk around and enjoy. In the past, they've hosted giant wooden bugs and massive LEGO creations, both kid approved! When visiting, bring sunscreen, swimsuits, towels, and clothes to change into after getting wet. Be sure to bring water bottles and pack a lunch if you want to spend the day there.

Klehm Arboretum & Botanic Garden is a part of the Museums for All program, an initiative that allows any individual or family that receives SNAP benefits (such as EBT or WIC) to visit Klehm at no charge by showing their card upon entry.

DOTY SPRAYGROUND

365 W Locust St., Belvidere
belviderepark.org/location/doty-park

Head east to enjoy another fun splash pad at Doty Park. Doty Sprayground is open daily from late May to September and is completely free to visit. The Sprayground includes geysers, a water tunnel, spinning water pole, and other features that kids can interact with. Be sure to spend some time at the playground directly across the parking lot from the Sprayground. After spending the day in the water, take a short walk to Sips & Sprinkles or Dari Ripple to enjoy some ice cream. Both are within walking distance of the park.

How to be a best mom:

- **Take a walk on the Kishwaukee Riverfront path located across from the park.**
- **Head over to Bob's Park (400 Meadow St.) for another fun playground.**

VARIETY OF SPRAY POLES

Throughout Rockford

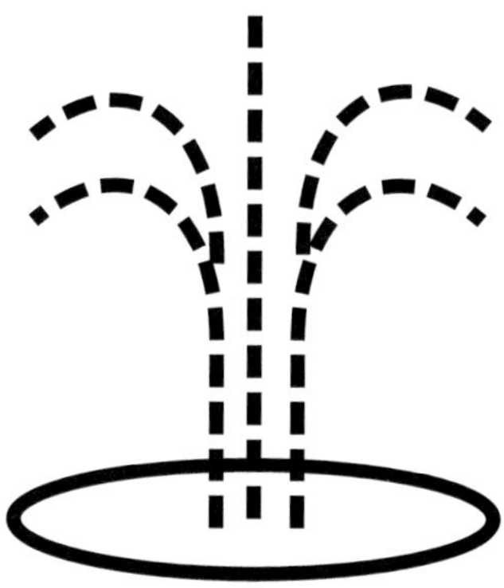

For a quick cool-off, there are a variety of spray poles throughout Rockford. These poles are often located at local playgrounds and offer kids a way to beat the heat without the frills. Spray poles can be found at Beattie Playground, Black Hawk Park, Bloom School Playground, Brown Park, Churchill Park, Ekberg-Pine Manor, Harmon Park, Highland Park, Keye-Mallquist Park, Liberty Park, Mandeville Park, Sabrooke Playground, South Henrietta Park, and Washington Park. Most spray poles have a button to activate the water feature while others are automatically activated when the temperature is above 95 degrees. Kids love the quick shower of cool water on a hot day!

How to be a best mom:

- **Bring your skateboards to enjoy the skate park in Washington Park.**
- **Check out the Native American mounds in Beattie Park.**

Best Place to Find Your Zen

ANDERSON JAPANESE GARDENS

318 Spring Creek Rd. | 815-229-9390
andersongardens.org

Escape the hustle and bustle of daily life and find peace at Anderson Japanese Gardens. The nationally recognized Japanese gardens were built in 1978 after John Anderson was inspired by a visit to the Portland Japanese Garden. The gardens were graciously donated and turned into a nonprofit entity in 1998 so the public could enjoy the beauty that the Andersons had cultivated. Anderson Japanese Gardens is open from May through October each year. They offer a donation day once per month at a discounted rate.

Anderson Japanese Gardens spans more than 12 acres and includes several distinct areas. The gardens were meticulously planned to take advantage of the land available and make it appear much larger. The gardens are a place of tranquility and beauty that all ages can enjoy. A short hike along the pathway leads to beautiful Japanese-style bridges and two waterfalls, one on each side of the property. There is also a large lagoon with several lovely statues overlooking the water.

Throughout the year, Anderson Japanese Gardens hosts family-friendly events including a festive Trick or Treat, holiday light show, outdoor concerts, summer camp, and a Japanese Festival. The Japanese Festival is a two-day event, usually held in July, that includes traditional Japanese tea ceremonies, live music, dance performances, and vendors. Fresco at the Gardens, located on the grounds of Anderson Japanese Gardens, is a peaceful place to have brunch with a gorgeous view. A great time to visit is in the fall when the gardens display magnificent colors.

KLEHM ARBORETUM AND BOTANIC GARDEN

2715 S Main St. | 815-965-8146
klehm.org

Make a trip to Klehm Arboretum to spend some rejuvenating time in nature. Klehm has nearly two miles of paved paths and three miles of wooded trails for the whole family to explore. Klehm has a variety of plant life not seen in any other natural area in the United States due to experimental planting in the early 1900s. Klehm is open from mid-May to early October each year and has a small admission fee to enter.

How to be a best mom:

- **Visit during the summer or early fall to check out traveling exhibits in the gardens.**
- **Bring your swimsuits to enjoy the Kids Creek and splash pad.**

MARTIN PARK

5600 Park Ridge Rd., Loves Park | 815-987-8800
rockfordparkdistrict.org

Located on the banks of the Rock River, Martin Park in Loves Park offers a tranquil place to walk by the water and enjoy the beauty of nature. The park cover 18 acres and includes a nearly 3-mile trail that crosses into Rockford, passes through Sportscore One, and ends near the Winnebago County Forest Preserve Headquarters. The path includes a wooden bridge which kids will love to ride their bikes on as well as several docks where you can get a closer view of the water.

How to be a best mom:

- **Take a hike on one of the wooded trails.**
- **Pack a lunch to enjoy at the picnic tables near the playground.**

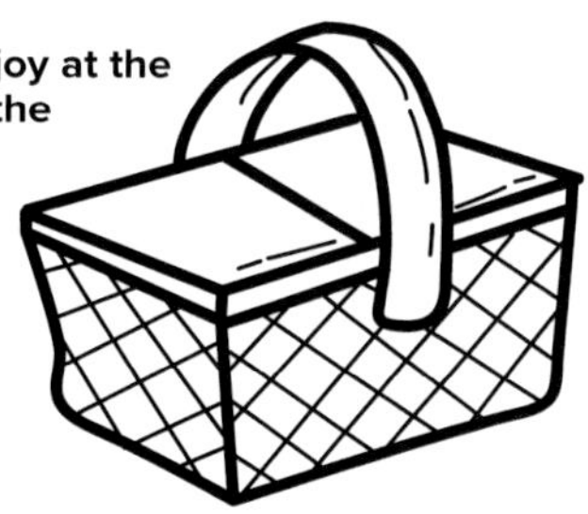

Best Place to Welcome Spring

NICHOLAS CONSERVATORY & GARDENS

1354 N 2nd St. | 815-987-8858
nicholasconservatory.com

Buds on the plants at Nicholas Conservatory & Gardens are one of the first signs of spring in Rockford! The gardens have welcomed spring since the Sinnissippi Gardens were planted alongside the Rock River in 1924. The outside of the gardens has walking paths, public art including the famous *Sight Seeing* statute of a man taking a photo, the Eclipse Lagoon, and several gardens including a large rose garden with 62 varieties of roses. Families can explore the exterior gardens for no cost. A small admission fee is charged to enter the conservatory.

Inside the Nicholas Conservatory, there are hundreds of tropical plants including orchids, banana trees, and mango trees as well as a man-made stream full of koi fish. In the spring, Nicholas hosts an annual butterfly exhibit where kids can learn about a butterfly's life cycle before entering a butterfly enclosure and feeding dozens of butterflies with sugar water. It's an amazing way to get an up-close look at some of nature's most beautiful insects.

The outdoor gardens come alive in the spring with thousands of roses and other local plant life as well as the return of the two swans that call the Eclipse Lagoon home. During one of the monthly family outdoor nature hikes, it's not unusual to spot ducks, squirrels, and other creatures welcoming spring.

ROCK RIVER RECREATION PATH

Spring is a great time to dust off those bikes and scooters and get outside for some time on the trails! Rockford has a variety of paved recreation paths including the biggest in the area, the Rock River Recreation Path, which spans over 10 miles from downtown Rockford to the surrounding city and village of Loves Park and Machesney Park. Additional paths can be found in Cherry Valley between Swanson Parkway and Valley Woods (1.43 miles) and in Rockford along Kent Creek between Talcott-Page and Lockwood Parks (3 miles).

✓ *How to be a best mom:*

- **Stop at Butler Park in Cherry Valley to play on vintage playground equipment.**
- **Take a photo with the Rockmen Guardians on the Rock River Recreation Path.**

RICHARDSON FARM TULIP FESTIVAL

909 English Prairie Rd., Spring Grove | 815-675-9729
richardsonadventurefarm.com

Take a drive to Richardson Adventure Farm for a special festival for flower lovers in the spring! Their annual Tulip Festival features over one million tulips in a variety of colors, making it one of the largest tulip festivals in the Midwest. Throughout the fields, there are adorable photo opportunities where you can get great pictures of your kids. Kids will also love picking a tulip to take home with them. In addition to the tulip fields, the festival also features live music and food trucks. There are yard games like cornhole that families can play together too.

✓ *How to be a best mom:*

- **Pay a few dollars more to cut an entire bouquet of tulips to take home.**
- **Plan a visit to Richardson Farm during the fall for pig races, corn mazes, and lots of fall fun.**

Best Place to Experience Nature

ROCK CUT STATE PARK

7223 W Lane Rd., Loves Park
815-885-3311
dnr.illinois.gov/parks/park.rockcut.html

Camp, fish, boat, and enjoy nature's beauty at Rock Cut State Park! This park encompasses 3,254 acres of land including two lakes—Pierce and Olson Lakes. Pierce Lake offers boating and fishing while Olson Lake includes a swimming beach. The park is packed with more than 40 miles of hiking, horseback riding, cross-country skiing, and mountain biking trails. Wildlife including waterfowl, foxes, deer, beavers, woodchucks, and raccoons call the park home. There are more than 100 types of wildflowers in the spring and dozens of trees that burst into a multitude of colors each fall.

Kids of all ages will enjoy walking on the interesting and winding paths in the park. Families can take several easy loops, including the trail that winds around Olson Beach. One of the most popular activities at Rock Cut State Park is fishing! Pierce Lake is full of largemouth bass, bluegill, catfish, and more. A kids' fishing pond is planned to open in 2024. Families can also enjoy a picnic at one of the five rentable shelters complete with outdoor stoves and pit toilets.

During the summer, Olson Beach is a fun place to go swimming. The beach has boats, stand-up paddleboards, and kayaks available for rent. A concession stand sells ice cream, snacks, and beach toys. For a bigger meal, check out the Lone Rock Café. Families can also go camping at the park's 270 premium campsites or rustic cabin. Rock Cut State Park is a gorgeous place to enjoy the outdoors no matter what the season!

HONONEGAH FOREST PRESERVE

80 Hononegah Rd., Rockton | 815-877-6100
winnebagoforest.org/items/hononegah

Hear the call of the wild at Hononegah Forest Preserve. It is the oldest forest preserve in the county and offers beautiful scenery and a multitude of trails to explore. The preserve was once a camping area for Stephen Mack and Ho-no-ne-gah, Rockton's first settlers. Inside the preserve, there are thousands of towering trees including maples, white oaks, and hickories. Spend some time in one of the three shelter houses and enjoy a picnic or rent one of 57 campsites and spend a night under the stars.

✓ *How to be a best mom:*

- **Spend some time at the playground after a hike.**
- **Visit in the fall to see beautiful orange and yellow leaves.**

COLORED SANDS FOREST PRESERVE

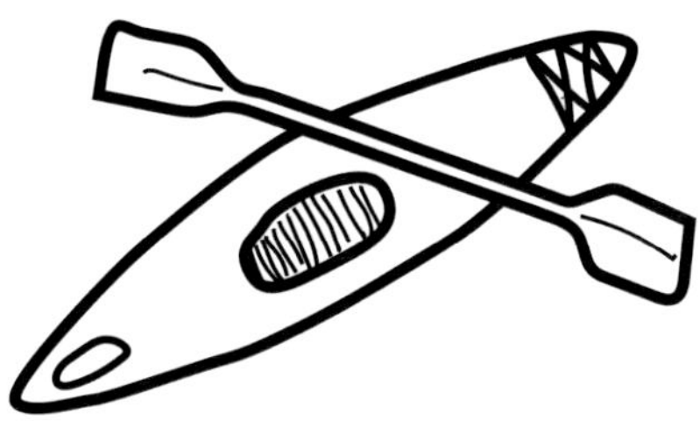

10602 Haas Rd., Rockton | 815-877-6100
winnebagoforest.org/items/colored-sands

Make a short trip to Rockton to experience the diversity of nature. The impressive 306-acre Colored Sands Forest Preserve is located along the Sugar River, where families can go tubing or kayaking during the summer months. The preserve is known for its bird life, unique rocks, and abundant wildflowers. Bring some binoculars to spot the larks, sparrows, American woodcocks, barn owls, and more feathered friends that call the preserve home. During the spring and fall, stop by the bird banding station to see birds being banded for observation.

✓ *How to be a best mom:*

- **Go tubing on the Sugar River during the summer.**
- **Search for lupine and shooting star flowers in the spring.**

Best Place for Free Outdoor Events

IN THE OUTDOORS PROGRAM

2685 New Milford School Rd. | 815-966-8747
atwoodpark.org

Enjoy educational and entertaining free events "In the Outdoors" at Atwood Park all year round! Atwood Park spans 334 acres of forest, prairie, and marshland and includes a portion of the Kishwaukee River. The park opened in 1957 and has been providing educational and memorable experiences ever since. The park is free to use, and open daily.

More than five miles of natural surface trails can be used for walking, biking, and cross-country skiing. Families are welcome to take self-guided hikes on the trails. Throughout the year, the Rockford Park District hosts free family-friendly events at Atwood Park. "In the Outdoors" events are geared toward education and awareness and have included activities like making a campfire, building a shelter, and identifying plants and wildlife. Atwood Park also hosts a popular annual Trick or Treat event in the woods each October.

One of the coolest things about Atwood Park is their Birds of Prey center. This unique exhibit features multiple birds of prey including owls, raptors, a vulture, a red-tailed hawk, and a bald eagle. Since 1988, Atwood has taken care of injured birds of prey that couldn't survive in the wild on their own. These birds are able to be viewed in their open-air outdoor enclosure that looks like a tree house. For a truly memorable experience, groups can stay overnight and bunk near the birds while sleeping under the stars.

NATURE AT THE CONFLUENCE

306 Dickop St., South Beloit | 815-200-6910
natureattheconfluence.com

Explore a little slice of nature right in the middle of a city at Nature at the Confluence. This hidden gem is located at the confluence of the Rock River, Turtle Creek, and Kelly Creek. The campus includes five acres of prairie, which bursts with color in the spring; trails; learning gardens including smelling and tasting gardens, which are a huge hit with kids; pollinator gardens; and more. Nature at the Confluence offers free or low-cost family-friendly programming throughout the year, and it's always free to explore the outdoors there.

✓ *How to be a best mom:*

- **Spend a summer evening at a bonfire or drum circle.**
- **In the winter, bring a sled to enjoy their small sledding hill.**

HOO HAVEN

10823 Cleveland Rd., Durand | 815-629-2212
hoohaven.org

Learn more about local animals at Hoo Haven. Hoo Haven is the area's only wildlife and reptile rescue and rehabilitation center. They offer a variety of open-house events that are both educational and entertaining for families throughout the year. The volunteers are dedicated to rehabbing sick or injured animals and releasing them back into their natural environment whenever possible. They offer free tours and themed events for holidays such as Halloween and Christmas as well as outreach programs for local schools.

✓ *How to be a best mom:*

- **Visit during September to see rehabbed bald eagles be released.**
- **Make it a special event by booking their private owl experience where you can get a photo with an owl.**

Best Place to See Something Unique

WOMANSPACE LABYRINTH

3333 Maria Linden Dr. | 815-877-0118
womanspace-rockford.org

Make it a day to remember by walking the labyrinth at Womanspace. This nonprofit offers programs for women, men, and children in creative arts, holistic health, interfaith exploration, and environmental stewardship. This includes youth programs geared toward drawing, photography, yoga, and more for ages 6 and up.

Womanspace's campus includes the main building where an art gallery and meeting space are located, the New Dimensions Studio for creative classes, and the Anjali Pavilion that hosts outdoor and social activities. Womanspace's labyrinth is a walking meditation path open to visitors of all ages. The labyrinth was created between 2000 and 2002 by a team of volunteers. Each stone was hand-laid to create a maze that is designed to be walked slowly and thoughtfully. Womanspace's labyrinth is the largest in the Rockford area.

The labyrinth can take up to 30 minutes or more to walk, depending on a person's pace. Walking the labyrinth is a great way for kids to practice patience, mindfulness, and focus. There are two benches located in the center of the labyrinth where kids can rest and reflect. Kids are also welcome to leave a symbol of their walk intention on the large limestone rock in the center of the circle. Please note, strollers will not fit in the labyrinth.

A great way to practice patience, mindfulness, and focus.

BEATTIE PARK

N Main St. between Park and Mound | 815-987-8800

Beattie Park is another spot in Rockford where families can view something quite special. Beattie Park is the home to three different types of Native American mounds—three conical mounds, an effigy mound in the shape of a turtle, and a linear mound. Effigy mounds are most commonly found in the Midwest. The mounds in Rockford were created in the Woodland period sometime between 700–1100 CE. The mounds were used for gatherings and rituals and are still a gathering place for Indigenous people today. Beloit College in Beloit, Wisconsin, also has a collection of more than 20 mounds.

✓ *How to be a best mom:*

- **Make it a whole day of fun with a stop at nearby Discovery Center Museum.**
- **Check out the Navy Anchor memorial dedicated to all who served in the Navy at Beattie Park.**

ROCKMEN GUARDIANS

1401 N 2nd St.

One of the most unique pieces of public art in Rockford is the Rockmen Guardians. Watching over the city, the Rockmen Guardians are located on the Rock River Recreation Path near the banks of the Rock River. These towering figures have been a staple of Rockford since they were created by a Milwaukee artist in 1987. Each statue is 12 feet tall and made completely of boulders weighing hundreds of pounds each. Be sure to stop and take a photo with these impressive works of art! They are one of many pieces of unique public art in Rockford.

✓ *How to be a best mom:*

- **Come up with names for each of the Rockmen Guardians, bonus points if they are rock puns!**
- **Take a walk down the Rock River Recreation path to see the other public art.**

Best Place to Feel like a Farmer

LOCKWOOD PARK

5201 Safford Rd. | 815-987-8809
lockwoodpark.com

Say hey to the horses at Lockwood Park! This park brings the charm of farm life into the heart of a big city. Open from May through September, Lockwood is free to visit but does offer some activities that have a small fee on weekends. Lockwood Park is one of the best places to play and make memories in Rockford.

Kids can run, jump, and play on Lockwood's multiple playgrounds. Kids can also pay a visit to Sarver Children's Farm, which is home to horses, goats, sheep, llamas, rabbits, and some ponies. Families can purchase pellets to feed the animals. There is also an observatory where kids can get a look at the moon and stars.

In October, Lockwood holds their annual Fall on the Farm event where kids can take a guided pony ride around the track, ride on a wagon through the fields and forest, walk through a corn maze, meet the animals in the Children's Barn, and pick their own pumpkins to take home. Lockwood Park gives families a chance to experience positive interactions with farm animals that they might not get to meet in everyday life. No matter what time of year, kids can enjoy a day of active play and appreciating farm life.

ALPACA PINES FARM AND FIBER MILL

21756 Beaverton Rd., Poplar Grove | 815-292-3222
alpacapines.com

Alpaca Pines Farm and Fiber Mill is an amazing place for a kid with a budding interest in farm life to explore. The family-owned working farm and fiber mill processes wool and alpaca fiber. They are also home to 42 alpacas, one llama, sheep, ducks, chickens, and one turkey. Private tours of the farm are available and events are held throughout the year including holiday shopping, farm hops, and fiber arts and crafts lessons.

✓ *How to be a best mom:*

- **Sign up your older kids and yourself to take a needle felting class.**
- **Visit during December to see Santa!**

FARMERS RISING

1545 Rockton Rd., Caledonia | 815-389-8455
farmersrising.org

Farmers Rising, formerly known as Angelic Organics Learning Center, is a place where kids and adults alike can learn how to build local food systems. Throughout the year, they hold farm programs and classes to teach people how to grow food and prepare it into healthy meals. In the summer, Farmers Rising hosts farm camps which allow kids ages 6–15 to experience life on a working farm by tending to animals, planting seedlings, pulling weeds, and preparing food.

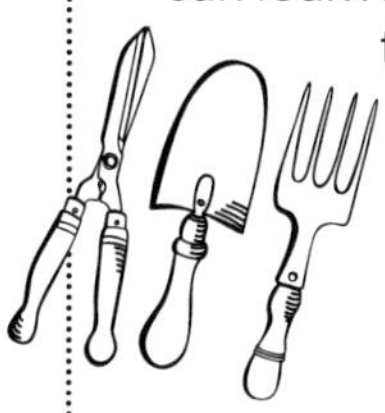

✓ *How to be a best mom:*

- **Sign up older kids to experience overnight camp where they get to sleep in cabins on the farm.**
- **Have a totally unique and unforgettable birthday party indoors or outdoors at the farm.**

Best Place to Get Dizzy

PAULYGROUND IN ALPINE PARK

950 Alpine Rd.
rockfordparkdistrict.org/alpine-park

Climb, spin, and swing at Paulyground in Alpine Park! Located near the intersection of Alpine and Newburg Roads, Paulyground in Alpine Park has multiple play structures for kids of all ages, unique spinning features, a sandpit, swings, and a roller slide. The playground is complemented by many mature trees in a beautiful forestlike setting. Alpine Park also has walking paths, picnic tables, and grills, and is home to Alpine Pool.

There are six distinct areas of play that kids under age 12 will enjoy. There's a baby section, toddler section, big kid section, sandpit, roller slide, and swings area. Babies will love the whimsical tree-themed playhouse, rocking ride-ons, and the music feature. The medium play structure is perfect for toddlers, who can enter the play structure by using steps or a climbing entrance to reach the low slides. Older kids will enjoy making themselves dizzy in the spinning cups, relaxing and gazing at the trees in the comfortable hanging chairs, bouncing on the two-person seesaw, and taking a spin on the large merry-go-round that can seat up to 10 kids comfortably.

Most of the playground is shaded so the equipment remains comfortable even through the hot summer months. Bring along a picnic for a lovely day at one of the area's best local playgrounds.

Multiple play structures for kids of all ages!

SINNISSIPPI PARK

1401 N 2nd St. | 815-987-8800
rockfordparkdistrict.org/sinnissippi-park

Take a spin inside the giant red ball at the big-kid playground in Sinnissippi Park for a wild ride! Sinnissippi Park has two great playgrounds, one for toddlers and preschoolers and the other for kids ages 5 and up. The big-kid playground has a variety of fun features including the spinning red ball where kids can see how long they can spin around before getting dizzy. Be sure to enjoy a calming walk on the paths throughout the wooded park afterward.

✓ *How to be a best mom:*

- **Keep an eye out for colorful fairy doors on the trees.**
- **Pack a lunch to enjoy at one of the shelters with picnic tables nearby.**

HIGHLAND PARK

3011 Rural St. | 815-987-8800
rockfordparkdistrict.org

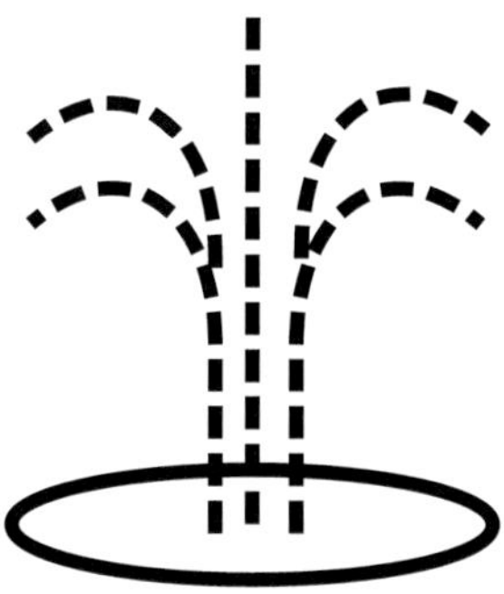

There are two different ways to get dizzy at Highland Park. First, soar through the air while holding onto a giant spinning top that allows kids to either sit inside and hold onto the rails or stand on the perimeter while someone spins the structure. Second, enter the giant spinning ball to get a double dose of dizziness. This playground offers Astroturf flooring and is mess-free at all times of the year. During the summer months, kids can cool off at the spray pole located just outside the playground.

✓ *How to be a best mom:*

- **Pack a towel so you can enjoy the spraypole in the summer!**
- **Playground hop to Dalquist Park a few minutes away to enjoy another playground.**

Best Place for Little Ones to Play Indoors

THE PLAY AREA IN CHERRYVALE MALL

7200 Harrison Ave. | 815-332-2440
shopcherryvalemall.com

Let your littlest adventurer explore and climb at the soft play area in CherryVale Mall. The play area is located on the lower level near the Tilted 10 entrance.

The play area is open daily during the same hours as CherryVale Mall. The space is for kids under 42 inches tall and primarily geared toward toddlers. Kids must remove their shoes and place them in cubbies before entering. The play area consists of multiple soft play structures that kids can climb on and through. The entire area is designed to mimic the outdoors. Kids can slide down a traditional double slide or an overturned log slide. They can balance on giant soccer, tennis, and golf balls and even crawl through the soccer ball.

Parents can relax on the cushioned bench seating around the perimeter of the space while watching their kids play. The area is not fenced in, but there is only one entrance in and out that parents can monitor. No food or drink is allowed in the area. After doing some shopping in the mall, playing at the play area is a great way to reward a little one.

TOT SPOT

711 N Main St. | 815-963-6769
discoverycentermuseum.org

When the weather isn't cooperating, the Tot Spot inside Discovery Center Museum offers another option for indoor play. The Tot Spot is geared toward kids 5 and under and includes several distinct imaginative play areas for little ones to explore. Kids can enjoy the newly renovated water play area with interactive features. They can pretend to be doctor and patient in the doctor's office, go grocery shopping in the store, play with the large train table, or pretend to go camping and fishing. Little ones will have hours of fun inside the Tot Spot.

How to be a best mom:

- **Be sure to visit the amazing outdoor playground during the spring, summer, and fall.**
- **Sign your little ones up for Tot Spot summer camp where they can make friends, have fun, and learn new things.**

TINY TOTS

4150 N Perryville Rd., Loves Park | 815-969-4082
saporaplayworld.com

Sapora Playworld has a play area made just for the tiniest climbers. The Tiny Tots section has a soft play structure with tubes to explore, slides, and climbing elements. Kids can also travel through a tunnel with soft hanging punching bags to maneuver around. The Tiny Tot area is located next to the bigger play structure, which is geared toward kids ages 5–12. Sapora is open daily and has a small admission fee.

How to be a best mom:

- **Spend the whole day there and go ice skating at the attached Carlson Ice Arena.**
- **Bring drinks and snacks that kids can enjoy in the lobby.**

Best Place for Big Kids to Play Indoors

SAPORA PLAYWORLD

4150 N Perryville Rd., Loves Park | 815-969-4082
saporaplayworld.com

Slide, climb, and play at Rockford's only indoor playground! Sapora Playworld is located inside Carlson Ice Arena. Sapora Playworld brings all the elements of an outdoor playground inside. Sapora is a popular place for birthday parties and offers several rental options. Admission ranges for kids, but parents get in free.

Sapora Playworld consists of two separate play areas for different age groups. The first area is geared toward toddlers and includes soft mats, hanging bags, and a few crawl tubes. It has bench seating near it, so parents can keep an eye on their little ones while they play. The second play area is much larger with equipment that reaches the ceiling. Kids ages 5–12 can climb and travel through the many tubes to reach different destinations in the play area and go down the giant three-person slide. The entire area is closed off, so parents don't need to worry about kids wandering.

Enjoy Rockford's only indoor playground!

Bathrooms are conveniently located in the play area, and water fountains are on-site. Within Carlson Ice Arena, there are a couple of food options including vending machines and a concession stand that is open select hours. Feel free to bring reusable water bottles and snacks to eat in the lobby. On select weekends, Rocky the Bear, Sapora's mascot, makes an appearance!

URBAN AIR ADVENTURE PARK

7137 E State St. | 779-243-0820
urbanair.com/illinois-rockford

For kids ages 3 and up who want to spend the day running, jumping, climbing, and swinging, Urban Air Adventure Park is the place to be! The facility is packed with fun activities for kids including trampolines, dodgeball, a ninja course, ball pit, indoor playground, climbing walls, and virtual reality games. Colorful lights, fun music, and an upbeat atmosphere make the place feel like a party every day. There is also a café with drinks and food to fuel up after a play session. Plan to spend several hours exploring!

✓ *How to be a best mom:*

- **Consider Urban Air for an unforgettable birthday party!**
- **Be sure to save the Urban Air specialty socks and bring them back each time you play.**

FLOW SUPREME AIR SPORTS

5505 E State St. | 815-255-3600
flowairsports.com

Kids who want to jump until they drop will love Flow Supreme Air Sports. It is the biggest trampoline park in the area with dozens of trampolines to choose from including incline trampolines, runways, and more. There is also a dodgeball and basketball area, aerial silks, foam pits, a balance beam, and more. Kids and parents can jump together, or parents can supervise from the seats throughout the facility while their kids play. Don't forget to pick up a cookie from Dirty Dough, located in Flow, before leaving!

✓ *How to be a best mom:*

- **Take a group photo in front of the shark mural before you go!**
- **Bring cash or card for the arcade games on site.**

Best Place for Discovery and Imagination

DISCOVERY CENTER MUSEUM

711 N Main St. | 815-963-6769
discoverycentermuseum.org

Let curiosity lead the way at Discovery Center Museum! One of the best kids' attractions in Rockford is the nationally recognized Discovery Center Museum, packed with more than 300 hands-on exhibits geared toward kids ages 12 and under. Don't worry, parents will also find fun things to do here, too!

The Discovery Center Museum has a multitude of hands-on STEAM activities, displays, and exhibits housed on two floors. The first floor includes a space section where kids can learn how to become an astronaut and view a planetarium show. An agriculture section has pretend animals to care for and farm equipment to try. This floor is also home to a crane, flight simulator, blocks, and even a bubble play area. The second floor has a Tot Spot for younger children that includes imaginative play areas like a kitchen, auto body shop, and camping site as well as a Maker Space for kids of all ages to create. A gated-off area has soft play toys and mats for babies and toddlers.

Throughout the year, the Discovery Center Museum hosts family events and traveling exhibits from children's museums around the country. After exploring the inside of the museum, head outdoors to run around the 8,500-square-foot outdoor space with a massive wooden playground, swings, a water play area, and secret garden. When visiting the Discovery Center Museum, plan to stay all day, have fun, and learn something new!

BURPEE MUSEUM OF NATURAL HISTORY

737 N Main St. | 815-965-3433
burpee.org

Burpee Museum of Natural History offers a variety of hands-on experiences for kids of all ages throughout their campus. On the lower level, kids can touch fossil replicas, make their own fossil rubbings, and learn about the history of dinosaurs in the greater Rockford area, including the famous teen T. rex, Jane. The third floor is also particularly interactive with animal pelts to feel, costumes to dress up in, and live reptiles to observe in the Sprouts room. Burpee also hosts story times and special events geared toward kids throughout the year.

✓ *How to be a best mom:*

- **Take the tunnel from Discovery Center Museum to Burpee to see the dinosaur murals on the walls.**
- **Visit in the summer to watch a free concert on their outdoor stage.**

MIDWAY VILLAGE MUSEUM

6799 Guilford Rd. | 815-397-9112
midwayvillage.com

Kids can interact with local history at Midway Village Museum. Inside the museum, there are a number of interactive displays including one featuring Rockford during the early 1900s. Kids can open cabinets and drawers in replica houses and buildings from the time period as they learn more about Rockford's history. Be sure to stop by the old-fashioned telephone booths where kids can listen to local leaders talk about immigration to Rockford. The annual Sock Monkey Madness event held in March is a chance for kids to sew their own sock monkey to take home.

✓ *How to be a best mom:*

- **Don't forget to visit the Doll House museum on site to see dozens of tiny replicas of houses throughout history.**
- **Plan a visit around Halloween to go trick or treating in the Victorian Village.**

Best Place for Dinosaur Lovers

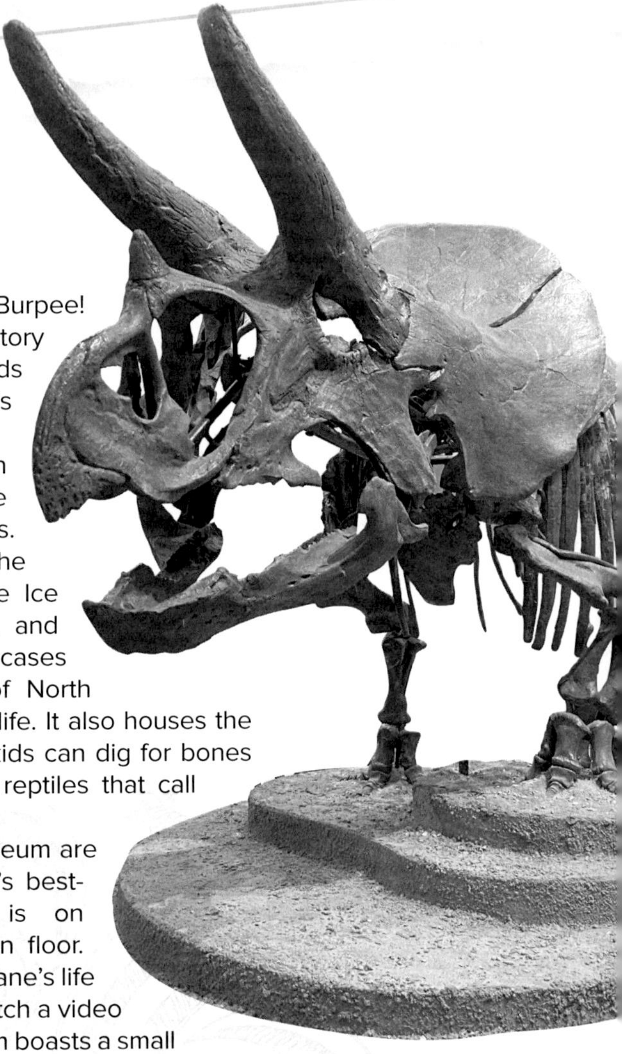

BURPEE MUSEUM OF NATURAL HISTORY

737 N Main St. | 815-965-3433
burpee.org

Dig into dinosaur history at Burpee! Burpee Museum of Natural History is another Rockford gem. Kids who love dinosaurs will adore this museum.

Creation begins on the main floor with a coal forest that once covered the entirety of Illinois. From there, you can head to the second floor, which covers the Ice Age as well as rocks, gems, and minerals. The third floor showcases lifeways of the first people of North America and displays local wildlife. It also houses the Sprouts Room, a place where kids can dig for bones and view the numerous living reptiles that call Burpee home.

The biggest draw for the museum are the dinosaurs! Jane, the world's best-preserved juvenile T. rex, is on permanent display on the main floor. Families can learn more about Jane's life in the interactive exhibit and watch a video about her last days. The museum boasts a small but mighty dinosaur section with skeletons of a triceratops named Homer among several others. Famous YouTube personality Mr. Beast even helped dig up a dinosaur fossil that can be seen on display at Burpee. Throughout the year, Burpee holds family-friendly events geared toward dino fans including their annual Paleofest where paleontologists from around the world speak about their experiences excavating fossils.

ROCK RIVER DISCOVERY PARK

711 N Main St. | 815-963-6769
discoverycentermuseum.org

Dino fans can experience the excitement of digging up buried dinosaur bones at Discovery Center Museum. In the Rock River Discovery Park, located outside of Discovery Center Museum and included in admission, kids can enter a large sandpit and dig to make some fantastic discoveries. Multiple dinosaur fossils are buried in the sandpit and tools are provided for kids to dig, brush off, and examine the uncovered bones. After digging up the dinosaur, kids can play on the massive playground.

✓ *How to be a best mom:*

- **Learn about dinosaurs closest relatives, chickens, in the agriculture section.**
- **Visit during the summer for themed events geared towards kids' interests.**

VOLO MUSEUM

27582 Volo Village Rd., Volo | 815-385-3644
facebook.com/volomuseum

Make a day out of dinosaur fun by heading to Volo, Illinois, for an up-close and personal dinosaur experience unlike any other. Jurassic Gardens in the Volo Museum allows kids to explore more than 45 lifelike animatronic dinosaurs. There are also hands-on and interactive experiences like dino digs, a prehistoric-themed playground, mining for fossils, photo ops, and a nine-hole mini golf course peppered with prehistoric creatures.

✓ *How to be a best mom:*

- **Check Volo Museum's Facebook page for special events like sensory Sunday where kids can enjoy a quiet dino park.**
- **Be sure to get a photo in the giant dino eggs!**

Best Place to Admire Art

ROCKFORD ART MUSEUM

711 N Main St. | 815-968-2787
rockfordartmuseum.org

Feast your eyes upon the works of talented artists of all kinds at the Rockford Art Museum! This museum is located in the Riverfront Museum Park, which houses Discovery Center Museum and Rockford Dance Company. The Rockford Art Museum is open select days from 10 a.m. to 5 p.m. with no admission fee.

The museum is known for its critically acclaimed Spiezer Collection, which is the most significant collection of Chicago art, inside or outside the city. Each spring, the Rockford Art Museum hosts the Young Artist Show, which showcases the works of talented elementary, middle school, and high school students from the greater Rockford area. The Young Artist Show has been a Rockford staple since 1941. The Young Artist Show includes art from students within a 50-mile radius of Rockford.

Throughout the year, the Rockford Art Museum holds monthly Cartoon Clubs, where kids are taught how to draw animals and people. They also offer summer camps for kids in kindergarten through fifth grade instructed by local artists. These camps have fun themes that kids enjoy like squishy art, superheroes, and Kawaii. The Rockford Art Museum also has a beautiful gift shop with many unique, artistic, and original items that would make wonderful gifts.

J. R. KORTMAN CENTER FOR DESIGN AND KORTMAN GALLERY

107 N Main St. | 815-968-0123
jrkortman.com

Another place to view fine art is J. R. Kortman Center for Design and Kortman Gallery. The space is both a store with unique and wonderful artistic gifts as well as a gallery that showcases local artists and swaps out artwork every few months. Older kids will enjoy the displays, which often feature local artists and have a theme such as Liberman Red, which honored the 45th anniversary of the *Symbol* sculpture. Don't forget to stop in the gift shop where a variety of unique *Symbol* gifts, and other Rockford landmark items, are sold.

✓ *How to be a best mom:*

- **Make a stop in the gift shop for one of a kind gifts for kids including puppets.**
- **Make a family tradition out of collecting the hand-painted Rockford landmark Christmas ornaments each year.**

317 ART COLLABORATIVE

317 Market St. | 815-272-0411
317art.org

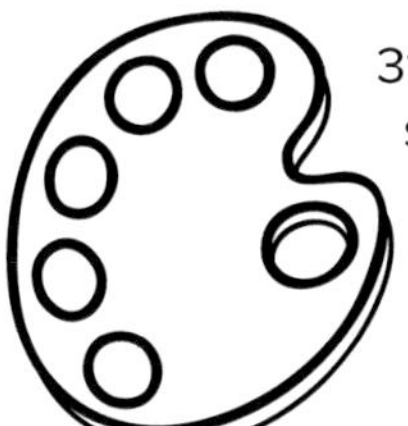

317 Art Collaborative hosts numerous gallery shows throughout the year, many of which are appropriate for kids to view. The themed shows highlight local artists working in a variety of mediums including painting, photography, sculpture, and more. On Saturday mornings throughout the year, 317 Art Collaborative gives kids the chance to create their own artwork at SmARTy Pants Art Studio, located inside the 317 building. Kids complete a different project each week, often themed with the time of year, and learn new art techniques and styles at each class.

✓ *How to be a best mom:*

- **Drop the kids off for a morning of artistic fun on Saturdays then have a delicious breakfast at one of the nearby restaurants**
- **Sign your kids up for summer camp where they'll learn a variety of art techniques and styles.**

Best Place to Step Back in Time

TINKER SWISS COTTAGE

411 Kent St. | 815-964-2424
tinkercottage.com

See what life was like at the turn of the century at Tinker Swiss Cottage! Once owned by the Tinker family, this house has been a museum since 1943. It is one of the only remaining Swiss-style homes in the US. The cottage has been lovingly preserved to feel as if visitors are stepping back in time when they enter it. The 27-room, three-story cottage is a popular field trip destination.

Inside Tinker Swiss Cottage, families can take a guided tour, which includes information about the Tinker family, the home, and the Victorian period. The main level includes a decorated sitting room, dining room, kitchen, and a beautiful round library with a spiral staircase. The house is filled with ornate woodwork, intricate murals, and antique items that the Tinkers used while living there. Touring the home gives kids a chance to learn about what life was like at the turn of the century for a wealthy Rockford family.

Throughout the year, Tinker Swiss Cottage hosts events including tea parties and haunted tours. One of the most popular things about the cottage is the rumor that it is haunted by its former inhabitants. The house has had numerous ghost hunters, spiritual mediums, and even several television shows visit to try to determine whether spirits remain there as well. Is it haunted? Take a tour and judge for yourself!

MIDWAY VICTORIAN VILLAGE

6799 Guilford Rd. | 815-397-9112
midwayvillage.com/midway-village-tours

During the spring, summer, and fall, families can be transported back to the late 1800s as they explore Midway Village Museum's outdoor Victorian Village. Spanning 13 acres, Victorian Village includes 19th-century gardens and 26 historical buildings filled with artifacts and antiques from the time. Kids will love seeing the difference between a store in modern times and a general store in the 1800s. During special events, historical interpreters can be seen playing villager roles such as banker and blacksmith in the village.

How to be a best mom:

- **Be sure to check out the historical accurate outdoor gardens filled with flowers during the Spring and Summer.**
- **Get family photos taken at the popular Woodward Millhouse located on the edge of the property.**

LAURENT HOUSE

4646 Spring Brook Rd. | 815-877-2952
laurenthouse.com

Take a tour to experience the wonder of a Frank Lloyd Wright creation right here in Rockford and step back into the 1950s! Rockford is home to the only dwelling Frank Lloyd Wright ever designed for a person with a disability. The beautiful Laurent House was built in 1952 to accommodate owner Kenneth Laurent's wheelchair and allow him to move freely throughout the space. Today, the historic home is filled with well-preserved mid-century furniture and original Wright-designed lighting and can be toured throughout the spring, summer, and fall.

How to be a best mom:

- **Make a day out of it by taking a joint tour of the nationally recognized Anderson Japanese Gardens and Laurent House.**
- **Sign up older kids with an interest in architecture for summer camp at Laurent House.**

Best Place to Learn about Rockford's History

MIDWAY VILLAGE MUSEUM

6799 Guilford Rd. | 815-397-9112
midwayvillage.com

Learn about Rockford through the ages at Midway Village Museum! This museum has seven exhibition galleries with more than 110,000 items in their collection. They also have an outdoor Victorian Village where reenactors host special events throughout the year.

Inside the museum, kids will enjoy the sock monkey section, which showcases the history of the iconic Nelson Knitting Company "Rockford Red Heel" sock. There are numerous sock monkeys on display, including the six-foot-tall Nelson. There are also several hands-on exhibits designed to look like historical kitchens, living rooms, grocery stores, and shops that kids will enjoy exploring. Another fun exhibit is the miniature dollhouse building, filled with dollhouses from different periods and cultures. There is also a large exhibit about the famous Rockford Peaches.

Outside, the Victorian Village consists of 26 buildings that have been created or restored to what they looked like in Victorian times. Some buildings were rescued from demolition and brought to the Victorian Village. The village includes a one-room schoolhouse, church, general store, blacksmith, hospital, and more. Throughout the year, Midway Village hosts several family-friendly events including a Trick or Treat through the Victorian Village and a large World War II reenactment. Special events typically include historical reenactors and demonstrations of blacksmithing and other old-timey activities.

ERLANDER HOME MUSEUM

404 S 3rd St. | 815-963-5559
swedishhistorical.org

In the mid-1800s, the Swedish population boomed in Rockford. The Erlander Home Museum offers a chance to learn about the history of Rockford's Swedish population. The home was built in 1871 and is located in the historic Haight Village, which was one of the first established settlements in Rockford. The home hosts a collection of Rockford-made furniture and artifacts from Swedish immigrants. Tours are offered from May through September and also by appointment.

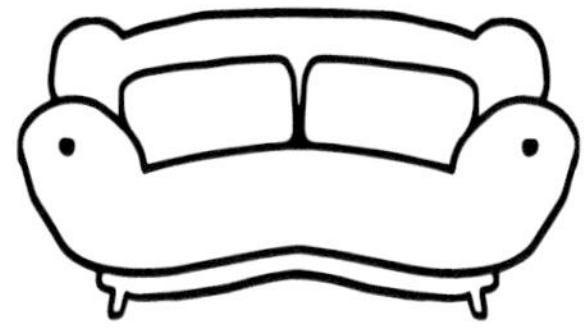

How to be a best mom:

- **Have an authentic Swedish breakfast or lunch at Stockholm Inn or Swedish Pancake House after visiting the museum.**
- **Sign up for a Swedish folk painting class held at the museum throughout the year.**

ETHNIC HERITAGE MUSEUM

1129 S Main St. | 815-962-7402
ethnicheritagemuseum.org

Families can learn the stories and traditions of the earliest settlers of the city at the Ethnic Heritage Museum. It includes six galleries that focus on the first immigrant groups that settled in the Rockford region. The galleries are organized into the following categories: African American, Hispanic, Irish, Italian, Lithuanian, and Polish. The galleries showcase items from these ethnic groups including early Rockford maps, vintage clothing, artifacts, and more. Right next door, the Graham-Ginestra House is an 1857 preserved home full of Victorian-era artifacts that families can tour.

How to be a best mom:

- **Museum hop to Tinker Swiss Cottage for a day of historical education.**
- **Visit on select dates in the spring to enjoy a historical teatime.**

Best Place to See Classic Cars

HISTORIC AUTO ATTRACTIONS

13825 Metric Rd., Roscoe | 815-389-7917
historicautoattractions.com

Motor into Historic Auto Attractions for classic cars and so much more! Located in Roscoe, Illinois, Historic Auto Attractions is one of the largest private museums in Northern Illinois. Historic Auto Attractions boasts 90,000 square feet packed with antique and classic cars, memorabilia, artifacts, and more.

Historic Auto Attractions has 25 exhibits including a 9/11 memorial, a section on Elvis Presley, a collection of Prohibition-era vehicles and memorabilia, the Hall of Presidents, a NASA space exhibit, and the world's largest collection of presidential and world leaders' limousines. The museum also houses one of the most extensive collections of Kennedy family artifacts in the United States. The museum adds attractions frequently so there's always something new to see.

Kids will enjoy the animal kingdom with taxidermy animals from the Arctic, the Great North, and the Serengeti. Animals on display include a polar bear, wolves, lions, and bears. Another kid favorite is the Bigfoot Monster Truck. This display awes and amazes with the sheer size of the monster truck's tires! Kids will also enjoy seeing vehicles from classic cartoons and movies such as the Batmobile, Ecto-1 Ghostbusters car, a DeLorean, and the Flintstones car from the *Flintstones* movie! When visiting, expect to spend several hours exploring, reading about each exhibit, or taking a tour from the very knowledgeable staff.

VINTAGE WINGS & WHEELS MUSEUM

5151 Orth Rd., Poplar Grove | 815-547-3115
wingsandwheelsmuseum.org

Get up close with flying and driving antiques at Vintage Wings & Wheels Museum in Poplar Grove. The museum is dedicated to transportation created between 1903 and 1957 and houses both vintage cars and airplanes. The museum is located at the Poplar Grove Airport which also hosts fly-in events in the spring and summer. There are several early 20th-century airplane hangars and automotive garages where families can view classic cars, a vintage gas station, and more.

✓ *How to be a best mom:*

- **Take a picture with Jenny, America's first mass produced plane.**
- **Plan a visit around Christmas to visit Santa at the museum and see him fly in.**

KATIE'S CUP

502 7th St. | 815-986-0628
katiescup.com

Head to a Cars and Coffee event in Rockford from May through October to see a staggering collection of the area's best classic cars and meet the owners who keep them in pristine condition. Car shows are held at Katie's Cup the first Saturday of the month and include more than 200 cars at most events. These events are family friendly and often include appearances by local mascots like Hammy the IceHog, live music, giveaways, and more.

✓ *How to be a best mom:*

- **Be sure to get a photo with the massive monster truck that makes regular appearances at the event.**
- **Bring a book and enjoy some coffee inside Katie's Cup.**

Best Place to See History Come to Life

MACKTOWN LIVING HISTORY

2221 Freeport Rd., Rockton
815-624-4200
macktownlivinghistory.com

Witness history come to life at Macktown Living History! Located in Macktown Forest Preserve, Macktown Living History has the distinction of being Winnebago County's earliest settlement. The settlement was founded in 1835 by fur trader Stephen Mack and his Native American wife, Ho-no-ne-gah, whom the Rockton high school is named after.

Visitors can tour Stephen Mack's carefully restored home, which rests near the confluence of the Rock and Pecatonica Rivers, as well as explore an original Whitman Trading Post building and Stevens' Woodworking Shop. The woodworking shop was also the area's first school. The Macktown Living History Education Center contains a variety of historic and prehistoric artifacts. Macktown Sundays are an opportunity for families to learn about aspects of living on the site throughout history, including native culture, archaeology, farming, gardening, and more.

The Gathering, an annual reenactment weekend each April, is one of Macktown Living History's biggest events. Dozens of reenactors demonstrate crafts, jobs, and more from the era. There is also a living history event in December, which shows how the early residents of Macktown would have celebrated the holidays in the 19th century. Throughout the year, there are special events, workshops, guided tours, and field trips including hands-on activities like spear throwing, creating fiber crafts, and cider making.

WORLD WAR II DAYS

6799 Guilford Rd. | 815-397-9112
midwayvillage.com

Each September, Midway Village Museum hosts WWII Days where families can get a sense of what it was like to live in a European village during the war. The museum is decorated with elaborate 1940s displays and the event boasts a huge military reenactment. This reenactment is the largest of its kind in the Midwest. Uniformed reenactors representing the US, Great Britain, France, Poland, Ukraine, Russia, and more tour in vintage tanks and other 1940s vehicles. There are also realistic battles with pyrotechnics that make families feel like they are part of the action.

How to be a best mom:

- **Take a walk around the LZ Peace Memorial Path next to Midway Village to see a Huey helicopter from the Vietnam War.**
- **Let kids spend the summer learning about history at Midway Village's summer camps.**

OLDE ENGLISH FAIR

1922 N IL Route 2, Oregon | 815-732-6111
strongholdcenter.org

The Olde English Fair held in October at the Stronghold Camp & Retreat Center is the place to experience a Renaissance Fair and be transported to the world of 16th-century England. The fair includes live performances, food trucks, artisan vendors, Vikings, royalty, horses, jesters, castle tours, and much more. It is truly an immersive experience and a great way for kids to get excited about history. Costumes are highly encouraged!

How to be a best mom:

- **Save some room in your stomach for the massive turkey legs!**
- **Visit the Knight's Encampment to learn the ways of a knight.**

Best Place to Experience Wildlife

SUMMERFIELD ZOO

3088 Flora Rd., Belvidere | 815-547-4852
summerfieldfarmandzoo.com

Meet the animals at Summerfield Zoo! Summerfield Zoo is the area's only place to see exotic animals. The zoo houses more than 50 species, including birds, reptiles, and mammals. Some of the fan favorites are the two-toed sloths, fennec fox, kinkajous, and pygmy goats. Summerfield Zoo is open May through October.

Summerfield Zoo is a more immersive experience than a traditional zoo. There are a variety of birds that roam the premises, giving visitors an up-close look. Many of the animal enclosures are open air, allowing visitors to see what the animal is doing. Summerfield Zoo offers special meet and greets with some of their most popular animals, including the sloths, which are available for an additional cost. In the summer, the zoo offers a hands-on summer camp where kids ages 6–12 can learn about the animals and help take care of them.

In the winter, Summerfield Zoo is transformed into Christmas Town, a reindeer farm with a festive holiday experience. During this special event, kids can visit the reindeer barn and meet several of Santa's famous flying reindeer. Then kids can go talk to the big man himself and tell him what they want for Christmas. The zoo offers hot cocoa and cookies during the event and puts on a reindeer flight school show a few times per day. Tickets for this event must be purchased in advance on their website.

SARVER CHILDREN'S FARM

5201 Safford Rd. | 815-987-8809
lockwoodpark.com

Lockwood Park offers a variety of ways to interact with animals! Sarver Children's Farm, located in the park, is home to goats, pigs, a cow, rabbit, ducks and a miniature Sicilian donkey named Dandy. Food pellets can be purchased so kids can hand-feed the animals. There is also a pony experience at the farm, which allows kids to groom, lead, and ride a pony or small horse. Kids who are interested in learning how to ride horseback can take lessons at Lockwood Park as well.

✓ *How to be a best mom:*

- **Sign up for summer camp for a week-long encounter with the animals at Lockwood.**
- **Be sure to take a photo with the giant cow statue near the playground.**

BIRDS OF PREY EXHIBIT AT ATWOOD PARK

2685 New Milford School Rd. | 815-966-8747
atwoodpark.org

Atwood Park has been a great place for kids to get a close look at powerful birds since 1988. The Birds of Prey exhibit is located in a rare accessible tree house. The birds are kept in open-air cages that kids can walk around to get a better look inside. Birds that live at Atwood include a bald eagle, turkey vulture, red-tailed hawk, and several owl varieties including an adorable tiny one! Each Saturday, the birds of prey are fed at 1 p.m. and the public is invited to watch.

✓ *How to be a best mom:*

- **Head inside the Atwood Lodge to see bugs and live reptiles on display.**
- **Check out the trench bunkers and target pit from when the property was Camp Grant during WWI and WWII.**

Best Place to Game On

NICKELWORLD

3321 N Main St. | 815-877-2771
nickelworld.com

Play a ton of games and save some serious cash at NickelWorld! This arcade is designed to give parents the most bang for their buck, charging an admission fee of $2.25 for everyone who enters the arcade and five cents for each game played. They also offer free, unlimited play on numerous classic games like Pac-Man. The center has more than 75 free and five-cent games as well as games that dispense tickets to trade in for prizes. NickelWorld has been a part of the Rockford community for more than 25 years.

NickelWorld has all the games families would expect to see in a traditional arcade as well as nostalgic favorites from the 1990s. They have an entire row of Skee-Ball games as well as an air hockey table where parents can challenge their kids to a game. They also offer classic racing games, carnival games, and claw machines that are filled with stuffed animals, jewelry, balls that can be redeemed for tickets, and more. There are several quick coin games where kids can insert a nickel and try to roll it into a slot for a chance to win tickets.

Need a place for your kid's next birthday? NickelWorld hosts 90-minute-long birthday parties with admission for up to 40 people, a free roll of nickels for the birthday child, and 100 free tickets. NickelWorld is open every day but Thursdays, but hours vary throughout the year. Check NickelWorld's website or Facebook page before going.

TILTED 10

7200 Harrison Ave. | CherryVale Mall | 815-491-8508
tilted10.com

Want to win a gigantic prize? Tilted 10 located in CherryVale Mall offers two floors of gaming fun. The 120,000-square-foot space has arcade games of all types including a huge variety of pinball machines. They also offer crane games packed with stuffed animals, candy, and tickets. There are sports games, virtual reality, air hockey, classic arcade games, laser tag, hyper-bowling, glowing mini golf, and more. Parents can load up reusable cards so kids can play all day.

✓ *How to be a best mom:*

- **Save time to play a round in the awesome black light mini golf courses.**
- **Get a sweet treat while you're there and try the cookie melt or homemade cookie ice cream sandwich.**

CORAL COVE FAMILY FUN CENTER

586 Progressive Ln., South Beloit | 815-543-4690
coralcoveffc.com

Head to South Beloit to find an arcade and indoor bounce houses at Coral Cove Family Fun Center. Coral Cove's games run off of tokens and dispense paper tickets that kids can trade in for awesome prizes. The arcade has more than 60 games including riding games, sports games, Skee-Ball, and air hockey. Prizes offered include stuffed animals, slime, candy, LEGO, and more. Coral Cove offers daily deals as well as parents night out on select weekends.

✓ *How to be a best mom:*

- **Check Coral Cove's Facebook page for a list of Parents Night Out where you can drop off kids for an evening of fun.**
- **Save the date for New Years Day when they have an annual balloon drop with prizes galore.**

Best Place for a Kid's Birthday Party

CHUCK E. CHEESE

3600 E State St. | 815-226-9400
locations.chuckecheese.com/us/il/rockford/3600-e.-state-st.

Make it the best birthday ever at Chuck E. Cheese! This popular chain has called Rockford home since 1988 and helped generations of Rockfordians celebrate birthdays in style. In 2022, it underwent a massive renovation; the animatronics were removed and replaced with more space for birthday parties and an interactive dance floor.

Bring the kids to Chuck E. Cheese for an updated version of the fun that parents experienced in their childhoods. Instead of worrying about each game's price, Chuck E. Cheese has created an all-you-can-play system. This allows parents to buy time on Play Passes that kids can use to play as many games as they want during the play period. They can also pause play at the front desk so kids can take a break. Families who download the app will receive special offers and seasonal deals.

Chuck E. Cheese has also upgraded its food! Their new pizzas include freshly baked mozzarella cheese and stuffed crust. They also offer wings, salads, and other appetizers fit for the whole family, with Buddy V's cake slices, churros, and giant cookies for dessert. Families can relax and enjoy their meal in comfortable booths. Birthday parties at Chuck E. Cheese are always a highlight of the year. Packages include game play, food, refillable drinks, and a spin in the Ticket Blaster for the birthday kid.

SAPORA PLAYWORLD

4150 N Perryville Rd., Loves Park | 815-969-4082
saporaplayworld.com

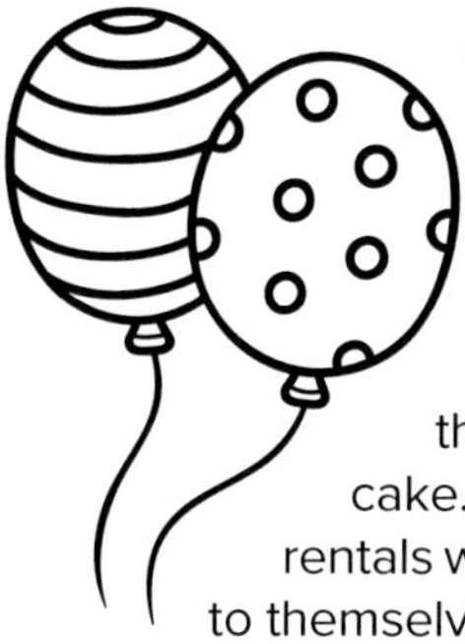

Kids who want to run and play during their special day would love a party at Sapora Playworld. Kids ages 12 and under can enjoy two indoor playgrounds, one for ages 5 and under and one for 5- to 12-year-olds. In addition, families will have access to a party room where they can bring their own food, drinks, and cake. Sapora is also available for private rentals where families can have the whole facility to themselves after hours.

✓ *How to be a best mom:*

- **Bring your own refillable water bottles and snacks to eat in the lobby.**
- **Visit on Monday and Wednesday all year for discounted admission.**

KIDS SPOT

9461 N 2nd St., Roscoe | 815-623-5437
www.kidsspot.com

Another awesome option for a party to remember is Kids Spot. These action-packed parties are held in the Kids Spot gyms and partygoers are encouraged to jump, run, climb, and play. Parties can be a basic theme or a Nerf or ninja theme. Kids Spot will provide the Nerf darts and partygoers need to bring their own blasters. A party room for food, drinks, cake, and presents is also included. The best part is that staff will handle the party activities leaving parents to kick back and relax.

✓ *How to be a best mom:*

- **Keep the kids entertained all summer at Kid Spot's all-day summer camp.**
- **Save for the date for Halloween when Kids Spot goes all out with a haunted house, trunk or treat, and costume contest.**

Best Place to Play Laser Tag

SECTOR 815

293 Executive Pkwy. | 815-580-3095
sector815.com

Get ready to let loose while playing laser tag at Sector 815! Sector 815 opened in 2023 in the former home of Laser Quest, a laser tag business that was open for nearly 30 years. Sector 815 took over the 7,500-square-foot space and made much-needed technology updates including sleeker weapons, more comfortable gear, and cool lighting effects. Sector 815 is open daily and is one of the largest laser tag arenas in the Midwest!

Sector 815 offers laser tags for ages 8 and up. Heavy vests are a thing of the past. Players now only need to carry laser guns and wear a sensor headband. The guns also have an updated look that makes them feel more realistic and include a recoil when shooting. If players really want to feel like they're part of the game, they can wear a bracelet that gives a shock when they are hit. Less realistic options are available as well.

Sector 815 offers over 30 different games styles including Infection, King of the Hill, Capture the Flag, and Free for All. Families can play a 30- or 60-minute session. Each player will get to create their own Call Sign (Gamer Tag) to track their stats and level up. Tweens and teens will particularly enjoy the fast-paced, high-stakes experience of playing a game at Sector 815. Sector 815 also offers birthday party packages starting at 12 people and an hour of play.

TILTED 10

7200 Harrison Ave. | CherryVale Mall | 815-491-8508
tilted10.com

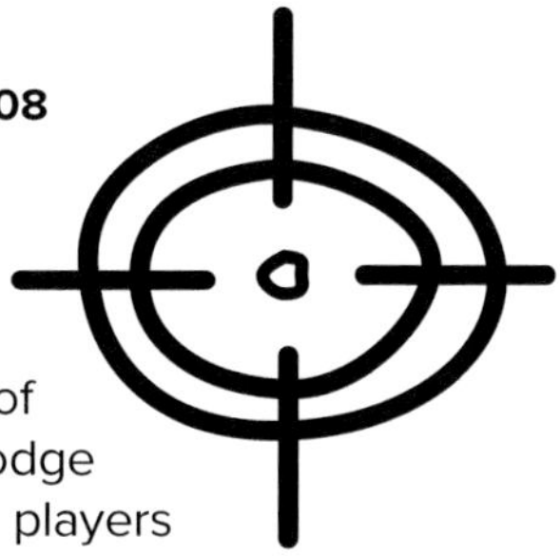

Titled 10 in CherryVale Mall offers a two-level black-light laser tag experience where the surroundings glow! Families can play a game of hide-and-seek behind obstacles while trying to dodge each other's lasers. The multilevel course allows players to attack from both above and below. There are a variety of game styles to choose from including Capture the Flag, Elimination, and more. Kids should be at least 6 years old and 42 inches tall to play.

How to be a best mom:

- **Head to the lower level to check out the dozens of pinball machines and play a game while you're there.**
- **Grab lunch, dinner, or snacks at their on-site restaurant and bar with kid's menu.**

VOLCANO FALLS

7602 Rock Valley Pkwy., Loves Park | 815-282-2100
volcanofalls.com

For a smaller, but still fun, laser tag experience, head to Volcano Falls. This awesome adventure park includes a massive mini golf course, go-karts, an arcade, snack bar, and batting cages. Inside the arcade, the laser tag arena looks like an alien land with plenty of places to dodge and duck. Kids can challenge their friends or parents to a fast-paced 10-minute round of laser tag. In addition to the laser tag game, kids can practice their spy skills and try to navigate their way out of a laser maze without touching any of the lights.

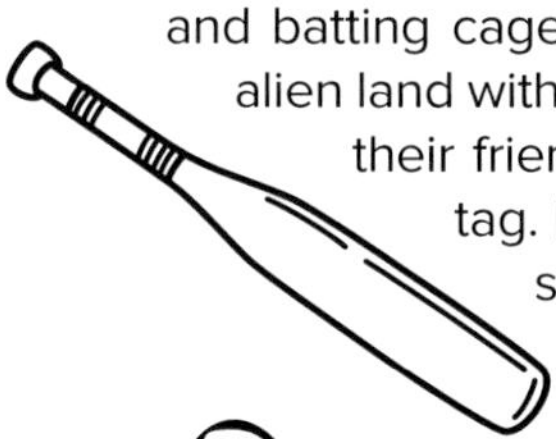

How to be a best mom:

- **Head outside for a competitive round of mini golf on Volcano Falls' signature volcano course.**
- **Check out the popular Ice Man water shooting arcade game while you're there.**

Best Place to Roller-Skate

SKATELAND

4843 Stenstrom Rd. | 815-874-6500
skatelandrocks.com

Roll on in for a good time at Skateland! This family-owned-and-operated roller-skating center offers public roller skating, rink rental, and birthday parties. This colorful and fun spot has been in business since 1992 and keeps the roller-skating tradition alive in Rockford with fun events all year long.

Skateland has colorful lights, fun carpet, and black-light paintings on the walls that glow when the arena enters party mode. Skateland offers open skating on select days throughout the year and has special skate times for homeschoolers. They offer both roller skate and rollerblade rentals, and have fixed skates for kids who are just learning. These skates' wheels take much more effort to turn so kids are less likely to fall. Skateland is also a popular destination for school PTO events. Skateland's hours vary so check their Facebook page or website before going.

Skateland has an on-site concession stand where families can get a snack and enjoy a soft drink or slushie. Many of the arcade games dispense tickets that can be redeemed for prizes. Skateland is a fantastic place to have a birthday party. They handle the decorations and table setup, and even sell goodie bags. They make having a party easy and fun. Kids will enjoy skating around the smooth wooden rink and listening to popular music. Plenty of tables, chairs, and benches are available for parents to spectate and kids to take a break.

SKATECO

3209 N Main St. | 815-877-4020
rockfordskateco.com

SkateCo is another classic Rockford establishment that has offered roller and in-line skating at their rink for the past several decades. SkateCo has a maple hardwood skate floor and offers public skating hours, birthday parties, skate rental, an arcade, and snack bar. SkateCo offers a Family Night skate on select Fridays and Saturdays throughout the year. Families can rent skates including fixed skates for first-time skaters. SkateCo plays upbeat popular music, has glow lights and brightly colored decor, and gives off a nostalgic vibe!

How to be a best mom:

- **Rent fixed skates for kids who have never skated before.**
- **Coordinate a skate night with your school's PTO.**

THE RINK AT PINE CREEK

6929 W Pines Rd., Mt. Morris | 815-946-9988
skatingfun.com

Take a drive to Mount Morris to try out the Rink at Pine Creek. The Rink is Northern Illinois's largest roller rink and has been in business for over 75 years. They are open every weekend and offer skating to top 40 music. The facility also has an arcade and snack bar. The Rink offers skate rental or allows families to bring their own skates. Zoom around their rink to colorful lights and a disco ball during their open skates!

How to be a best mom:

- **Plan a nostalgic birthday party that will keep kids active and entertained.**
- **Sign the kids up for summer skate camp where they can skate all summer long.**

Best Place to Jump Around

FLOW SUPREME AIR SPORTS

5505 E State St. | 815-255-3600
flowairsports.com

Jump into fun at Flow! Flow Supreme Air Sports was built in 2020 to offer Rockfordians a place to jump around. This trampoline park includes several unique stations and features. Admission prices vary per age, but all jumpers need to wear special socks to jump on the trampolines. Guardians who are not jumping get in free. Flow offers special sessions and rates for families, homeschoolers, and kids under age 6.

Kids of all ages will enjoy jumping around the main floor, which has more than 15 square trampoline sections connected by mats. Kids can get active in several areas including the gigantic free-fall pad where they can climb a set of stairs to a platform overlooking a blob-like mat filled with air. From there, they can jump onto their bottoms, do a flip, or jump backward.

The jumping continues at the foam pits. Kids can climb and swing on the aerial silks, race down a gymnastic mat that's perfect for flips, soar on a swing, and joust each other on a balance beam. Additional activities include a ninja course, a zip line, and a fenced-in section for trampoline dodgeball. Teens will also enjoy these attractions as well as the parkour course and slackline. Inside Flow, you can find Dirty Dough, a cookie company specializing in cookies with a gooey center.

CORAL COVE FAMILY FUN CENTER

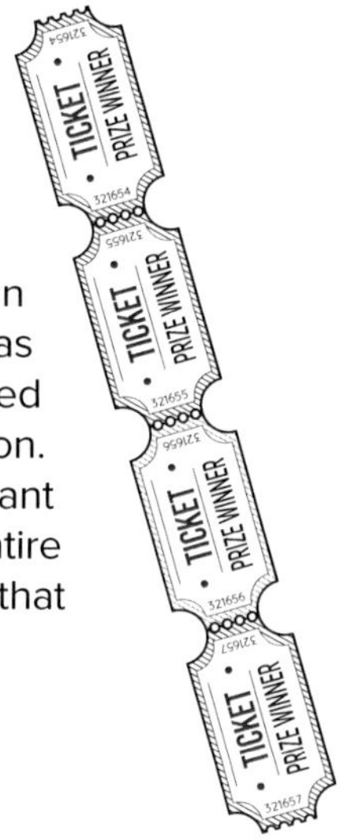

586 Progressive Ln., South Beloit | 815-543-4690
coralcoveffc.com

Kids can bounce and jump all day at Coral Cove Family Fun Center. Open all year round, Coral Cove Family Fun Center has an entire room dedicated to bounce houses, which are swapped out on a regular basis so kids don't get bored with the selection. Their bounce houses include mazes, obstacle courses, and giant slides. All bouncers require a wristband that is good for the entire day. The facility also has a full arcade with 70-plus games that dispense tickets redeemable for prizes.

How to be a best mom:

- **Experience jumping around virtually by playing one of their VR games.**
- **Drop the kids off on days off school for hours of play.**

STATELINE BOUNCE HOUSE RENTALS

815-980-6138 | statelinebouncehouserentals.com

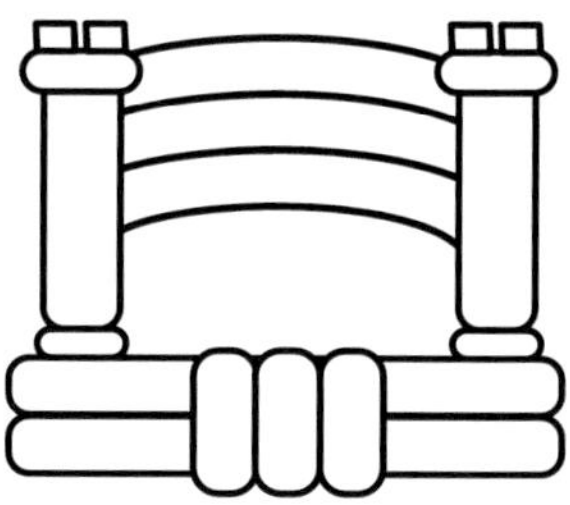

Bring the fun home by renting a bounce house from Stateline Bounce House Rentals. Stateline Bounce offers a huge variety of bounce houses including traditional enclosed bounce houses, radical 95-foot-long obstacle courses, double slides, and colorful castles. For hot summer days, they also offer water inflatables like slip-and-slides, 18-foot waterslide, and more. Stateline Bounce will drop off and inflate the bounce house and then pick it up after your day of fun is over.

How to be a best mom:

- **Add on a cotton candy machine or snow cone maker for an unforgettable party.**
- **Throw a carnival themed birthday party with the help of Stateline Bounce's many rentable games.**

Best Place for Daredevils

URBAN AIR

7137 E State St. | 779-243-0820
urbanair.com/illinois-rockford

Catch some major air at Urban Air Rockford! Urban Air is one of the newest kid-friendly attractions in the Rockford area. Urban Air is best suited for kids ages 5 and up, though there is a small indoor playground for preschoolers. Urban Air also requires purchase of their branded socks for play. Guardians get in free.

To start, they have three trampoline sections, in addition to netted-in dodgeball and basketball trampoline areas. The most unique trampoline attraction is the Wipeout game, which involves a spinning foam arm that kids must jump over before it hits them. Urban Air is more than just trampolines; they also have a four-lane ninja course that allows kids to scramble over obstacles and try to get to the end without falling into the ball pit below. They also offer virtual reality games and bumper cars.

The main draw of Urban Air is their harness sections. These areas are designed for kids to get a bird's-eye view as they complete challenges including an aerial obstacle course. While safely strapped in, kids can climb rock walls, balance on poles, and jump from a platform to fly 30 feet overheard. For most of the attractions, kids must be at least 36 to 42 inches tall. Urban Air also has a concession stand on-site with food, drinks, and seating for caregivers who want to relax.

SNOW PARK AT ALPINE HILLS

4402 Larson Ave. | 815-966-8737
alpinehillsadventure.com

In the winter months, kids can catch some air and do tricks at the terrain park at the Snow Park at Alpine Hills. This five-acre winter wonderland is only open between December and March, weather permitting. The snow park has two sections: the tubing area and the terrain park. Snowboarders can bring their own gear, or rent gear on-site, to use in the terrain park. The terrain park offers a few places to do tricks including boxes and hills.

✓ *How to be a best mom:*

- **Sign the kids up for snowboarding lessons at the park.**
- **Enjoy hot cocoa and snacks inside the lodge after you snowboard or go tubing.**

ROCKFORD SKATEPARKS

815-987-8800 | rockfordparkdistrict.org/skateparks

In the summer months, there are three skate parks to shred on in the Rockford area that kids can choose from: Churchill Park Skatepark, Flodin Boys and Girls Skatepark, and Harlem Community Center Skatepark. Each of the skate parks has a variety of equipment including big and small ramps, rails, boxes, stairs, and more. The skate parks are free to use and open to skateboarders, BMX riders, and in-line skaters.

✓ *How to be a best mom:*

- **Bring younger siblings to play on the soon-to-open new playground next to HCC Skatepark.**
- **Pack water and sunscreen because these skate parks are in full sun.**

Best Place to Mini Golf

VOLCANO FALLS

7602 Rock Valley Pkwy., Loves Park | 815-282-2100
volcanofalls.com

Putt your heart out at Volcano Falls Adventure Park! This family fun destination is one of the most eye-catching attractions in the Rockford area. Located just off I-90 in Loves Park, Volcano Falls boasts a giant volcano with water features that can be seen from the highway. With so much to do at Volcano Falls, both indoors and outdoors, there's no way anyone will say they are bored or want to go home.

The fun starts outside with the massive miniature golf courses. The Volcano Course is an 18-hole course featuring a climb up the volcano and a spectacular view of the whole park from the top. Volcano Falls also has two go-kart tracks outside. The Rookie Track, for riders taller than 40 inches, is a simple oval where kids can gain confidence in lower-speed cars. The Bridge Track offers more of a challenge with a few twists and turns and a ride over a bumpy bridge. Finally, the Slick Track offers a rapid-paced race that requires a valid driver's license to participate. Kids who enjoy baseball can take a turn in the batting cages.

Inside Volcano Falls, families will find a laser tag arena with a glowing Martian terrain. The indoor arcade has more than 50 games and a ticketless system that uses game cards. There is also a Virtual Reality Finger Coaster that kids and adults can ride if they dare.

One of the most eye-catching attractions in the Rockford area.

SYCAMORE FAMILY SPORTS CENTER

725 E State St., Sycamore | 815-895-7407
sycamorefun.com

Take a drive to Sycamore to visit Sycamore Family Sports Center for another outdoor mini golf experience. Their mini golf course is 18 holes with newly installed greens in 2022. The course has both challenging holes as well as some easier ones for younger mini golfers. The facility also has batting cages, basketball trampolines, soccer cages, a go-kart track, and a driving range. Families can easily spend a whole day here enjoying outdoor activities.

✓ *How to be a best mom:*

- **Stay for the whole day and get a discount bundle for all six family-friendly activities at the center.**
- **Swing by Ollie's Frozen Custard for some high quality frozen custard while you're in the area.**

TILTED 10

7200 Harrison Ave. | CherryVale Mall | 815-491-8508
tilted10.com

If the weather isn't cooperating or you want to mini golf in the winter months, Titled 10 in CherryVale Mall offers indoor mini golfing all year round. This is a special mini golf experience because the entire place glows! The two indoor courses are beneath black light and have reactive elements throughout. Choose to explore outer space or the ocean floor and golf through 18 holes with the family! Tilted 10 also offers hyper bowling, bumper cars, and a massive two-story arcade.

✓ *How to be a best mom:*

- **Make it a double and try both indoor courses in the same day!**
- **Try your hand at the massive claw machines with popular toys up for grabs.**

Best Place to Tumble

KIDS SPOT

9461 N 2nd St., Roscoe | 815-623-5437
www.kidsspot.com

Flip, cheer, and roll into fun at Kids Spot! Kids Spot is a 16,000-square-foot facility that houses two gyms and several studios for dance as well as a preschool. They believe that a healthy, active childhood is a building block to a successful life. Their smaller gym is geared toward younger visitors ages 5 and under while their main gym is good for kids over 5.

Kids Spot is best known for its lessons, which help kids build strength and flexibility and develop self-confidence. They offer lessons in gymnastics, tumble, and dance for kids of all ages. Kids who are crawling up to age 3 can attend gymnastics with a guardian. After age 3, guardians can take a seat in the stands and watch their kids progress.

Dance is available for kids ages 1½ to 18 years old in a variety of styles including ballet, hip-hop, and more. Cheer classes are designed for kids ages 4 and up to learn the proper techniques. Kids can also audition for competitive teams.

Kids Spot offers after-school care for students in the surrounding school districts, giving kids a chance to do their homework and then get active. Kids Spot also runs half- and full-day summer camps. Each week has a different theme and includes a field trip to a local attraction. Kids Spot is popular for birthday parties, which are fully staffed and managed by Kids Spot's staff so parents can kick back and relax.

GYMNASTICS ACADEMY OF ROCKFORD

6630 Spring Brook Rd. | 815-654-3867
gymnasticsacademyrockford.com

Gymnastics Academy of Rockford has been a staple in the Rockford tumbling and gymnastics community since 1977. Their large facility offers both recreational and competitive gymnastics programs for all ages. Gymnastics lessons begin at six months with a parent-child class. They also offer lessons in trampoline and a variety of dance styles through Miss Andrea's Dance. They host regular Parents Night Out where kids can be dropped off to enjoy a few hours of open gym, games, movies, and more. In the summer, GAR offers summer camps.

✓ *How to be a best mom:*

- **Let GAR take care of the birthday party activities and give your kid a fun and fast-paced party.**
- **Sign the kids up for active all-day summer camp which includes field trips.**

GAR NORTH

11447 N 2nd St., Roscoe | 815-623-2345
garnorth.com

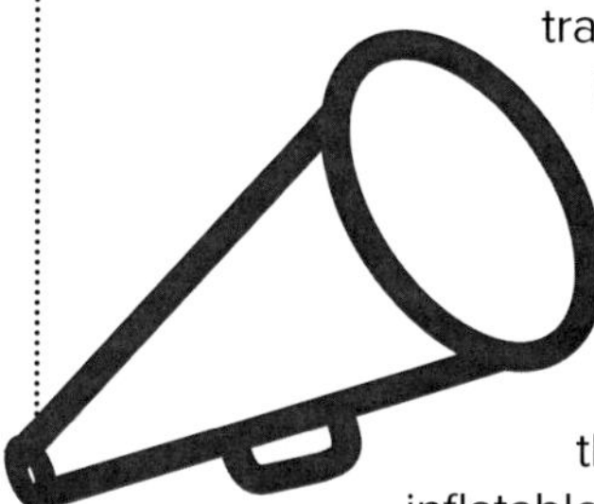

GAR North, located close to the Wisconsin border, offers tumbling, trampoline, gymnastics, ninja warrior, and cheer lessons. Recreational and competitive lessons are available for kids starting at 6 years old. Each child starts with a free trial class before signing up, and if they don't enjoy it, families owe nothing. GAR North also offers Parents Night Out and active birthday parties that give kids two hours to play on the Olympic trampolines, 70-foot Tumbl Trak, inflatable, and ninja warrior elements.

✓ *How to be a best mom:*

- **Schedule a no-risk trial class to see if your kid enjoys the sport before signing up for lessons.**
- **Spend days off school and breaks at GAR North's all day camps.**

Best Place to Paint Pottery

THE POTTERY LOUNGE

6059 E State St. | 815-977-3937
thepotterylounge.com

Unleash your inner artist at the Pottery Lounge! The Pottery Lounge is a family-owned paint-your-own pottery studio. No appointments are necessary, and they're open daily. They offer a large variety of ceramic and wood items as well as canvas to paint.

Families can enjoy getting creative in a friendly environment. Upon entering, you'll see a variety of items available that include things like figurines, mugs, banks, plates, and seasonal decor. The price marked on each piece is all inclusive. Families can use acrylic paint to decorate their piece and take it home the same day or they can have it fired and pick it up later.

The Pottery Lounge is a great spot to let kids get creative without worrying about cleaning up. They offer aprons to keep clothes clean and have a sink where kids can wash up. Kids as young as toddlers will enjoy painting with a brush or using their fingers to make their keepsake.

The Pottery Lounge offers ticketed themed events throughout the year, including ones geared toward kids' interests like Taylor Swift and Marvel characters. They also offer glow parties and other fun seasonal events for Halloween, Christmas, and more. Throughout the summer, they offer drop-off events for school-age kids to work on projects and have fun with friends.

Get creative in a friendly environment!

SIMPLY CERAMICS ROCKFORD

7104 Forest Hills Rd., Loves Park | 779-770-0418
facebook.com/1simplyceramics

A small studio with a homey feel, Simply Ceramics Rockford offers ceramic painting throughout the year. The business has a variety of ceramic items for sale including plates, figurines, vases, mugs, and more. They provide the paint and supplies needed to create a customized work of art. They also host events throughout the year and offer deals and specials. Simply Ceramics offers some of the lowest prices in the area.

How to be a best mom:

- **Check Simply Ceramics Facebook page for special events including schools out sessions.**
- **Make it a tradition to paint a Christmas ornament each year.**

MAKITY MAKE

101 N Johnson St., Woodstock | 815-334-2266
makitymake.com

Makity Make is another craft studio that offers ceramic painting among other artistic options. They have a selection of bisque-fired pieces including figurines, coin banks, boxes, mugs, dishes, and more. Prices on items include the cost of paint and materials as well as firing. They also offer to-go kits so you can take the items home to paint with your kids. In addition, they offer in-house workshops on a variety of mediums including clay building as well as art classes for kids.

How to be a best mom:

- **Throw your kids a unique birthday party by having a DIY paint party at Makity Make.**
- **Pick up a DIY Kids Kit for at-home painting fun.**

Best Place to Get Crafty

BRISTLE & TIMBER

6140 E Riverside Blvd., Loves Park | 779-970-6804
bristleandtimber.com

Get creative at Bristle & Timber! Bristle & Timber is a locally owned small business that offers a variety of DIY workshops where families can create beautiful works of art that they'll be proud to display in their homes. They are open daily.

Kids and parents can get crafty together at their fun workshops and special events. Every month, they hold themed walk-ins where families can create boards with a variety of stencils. Past themes include Lucky Charms for St. Patrick's Day, Harry Potter boards in October, and Christmas and gnome boards in December. They not only offer a variety of wood projects, but they also work with tie-dye, pillows, rugs, ceramics, and more.

Creativity is encouraged, but no special skills are needed. Bristle & Timber supplies the vinyl stencils, dozens of paint colors to choose from, and wood to work with. You can stop by a walk-in event and either make your creation at the studio or bring home a to-go kit. They have plenty of options for projects that both kids and parents will enjoy. They also offer private events and are a great spot for creative birthday parties, baby showers, and date nights.

THE URBAN ART STUDIO

Poplar Grove | 815-289-7853
theurbanartstudio.com

Throughout the Rockford area and beyond, the Urban Art Studio brings pop-up crafting, painting, and fiber arts events to local businesses. Workshops are held each month at different locations including the YMCA of Rock River Valley. Workshops include all supplies and teach kids and parents how to make a craft that they will complete that day. Past workshops have included macramé plant hangers, wall hangings, and more. The owner, Catherine, is a former elementary art teacher and offers workshops for all ages.

✓ *How to be a best mom:*

- **Check their Facebook page for upcoming seasonal events.**
- **Pick up a DIY bunny kit to make at home for a fun Easter craft.**

HAMMER & STAIN STATELINE

1406 Willowbrook Rd., Ste. 104, Beloit, WI | 608-291-7575
hammerandstainstateline.com

A quick drive over the state line to Hammer & Stain Stateline offers more opportunities for creativity. Hammer & Stain provides all of the materials needed to complete a project and instruction on how to do it. They offer board painting in addition to resin projects, knitting, and more. Kids love the popular squishy events where they can stuff their own cuddly animal and paint a ceramic to match. Events are held monthly throughout the year.

✓ *How to be a best mom:*

- **Check their Facebook page for special themed kid's workshops.**
- **Save the date for special winter themed projects during Beloit's annual Winterfest celebration.**

Best Place to Make Art

SMARTY PANTS ART STUDIO

317 Art Collaborative | 317 Market St. | 773-960-3195
smartypantsrockford.com

Create a masterpiece at SmARTy Pants Art Studio! SmARTy Pants Art Studio runs out of the 317 Art Collaborative. They host many events and gallery openings throughout the year in addition to kids' art classes. The studio participates in both the annual Spring and Fall ArtScene as well.

SmARTy Pants Art Studio offers kids a chance to get creative while learning new art styles. Every Saturday morning, the studio offers classes for kids ages 6 to 14. These art classes teach technique, critical thinking, focus, and art history. Each week has a different theme and kids leave class with a completed project to take home. Kids learn about customs around the world, which may include music, art, and food. Class size is maxed at 12 so each participant can get individual attention. Classes can be paid on a one-off basis or parents can purchase a six-class card. The studio also offers camps year-round. Birthday party packages are offered for groups of 10 kids or more.

Parents can drop off kids for the Saturday morning art class then head to Magpie for breakfast or grab a coffee from Inzombia and a muffin from Crust and Crumbles, all of which are within a few minutes' walk of the studio.

ROCKFORD ART MUSEUM

711 N Main St. | 815-968-2787
rockfordartmuseum.org

What better place to make art than an art museum? Rockford Art Museum offers several ways for kids to get creative. Cartoon Club is offered monthly for kids ages 6 and up. During this class, kids can learn how to draw animals, people, and more in a cartoon style. Each month has a different theme. Rockford Art Museum also offers summer camps based on different art techniques or styles like Kawaii. Often these camps are taught by local artists.

How to be a best mom:

- **Pay a visit in the spring to see the annual Young Artist Show where hundreds of talented local kids' artwork is displayed.**
- **Take the kids to the Greenwich Art Fair in September for a chance to create art and buy other artists' works.**

ROCK VALLEY COLLEGE'S WHIZ KIDS

3301 N Mulford Rd. | 815-921-7821
rockvalleycollege.edu/community/community-and-continuing-education/whiz-kids

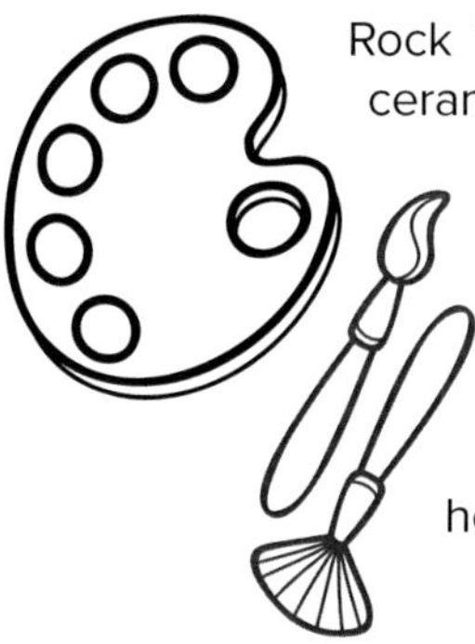

Rock Valley College's Whiz Kids program offers arts and ceramics classes for kids ages 5 and up. These classes are held throughout the year and focus on a different style of art at each meeting. Projects can include acrylic and watercolor painting, drawing, and multimedia work. Kids can learn about working in different mediums and discover their favorite way to express themselves through artwork. All classes are held on the Rock Valley College campus.

How to be a best mom:

- **Sign up kids who are interested in the performing arts for the StarBright children's theater production in the summer.**
- **Bring scooters or bikes to Rock Valley College to enjoy the paved walking path that winds through their campus.**

Best Place to Bowl

DON CARTER LANES

4007 E State St. | 815-399-0314
doncarterlanes.com

Bowl a strike at Don Carter Lanes! Northern Illinois's largest bowling facility, Don Carter Lanes has 42 lanes and offers bumpers for the youngest bowlers. Bowling shoes are available to rent, or families can bring their own. A variety of bowling balls are available to borrow including lightweight ones for kids.

They're open daily and offer open bowling times throughout the year. Setting up a game of bowling is quick and easy. Each game can take anywhere from 30 minutes to an hour depending on the group. If you get hungry while bowling, Shooter's Bar and Grill, located on-site, offers a full menu with burgers, pizzas, and wings. Seating is available by the lanes so families can watch each other bowl while eating.

Don Carter Lanes also offers cosmic bowling on select weekend nights where they turn on special lights and turn up the music. The atmosphere is fun and many items glow in different colors. During the summer, the alley participates in the Kids Bowl Free program where kids ages 15 and under can bowl two free games every day of the summer. (Shoe rental is not included.) Don Carter Lanes also offers kids bowling leagues throughout the year. Kids as young as 3 can learn.

PARK LANES BOWL

5318 N 2nd St., Loves Park | 815-877-6051
parklanesbowl.com

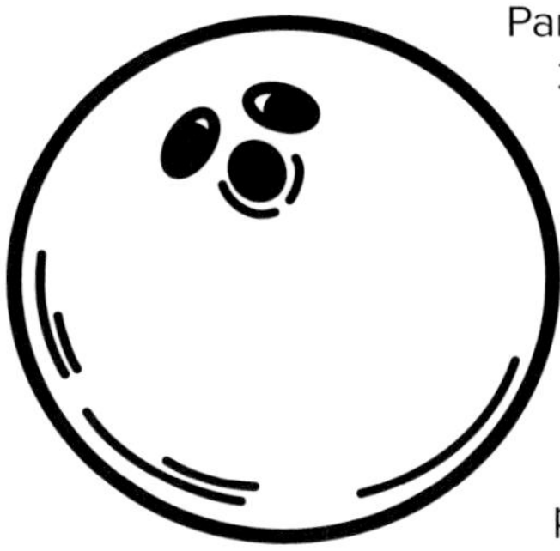

Park Lanes Bowl offers a modern bowling alley with 32 lanes including bumper bowling lanes. The bowling alley is open daily and has special events on holidays like Christmas Eve. They also offer cosmic bowling three times per week. Park Lanes Bowl often has deals for families to bowl for an unlimited amount during a set time frame. In addition, they offer kids' birthday parties that include pizza, pop, a bowling pin for the birthday child, and goodie bags.

✓ *How to be a best mom:*

- **Take a photo in front of the psychedelic flower mural in the Park Lanes parking lot.**
- **Head across the street after bowling for a delicious treat at Dairy Depot.**

VIKING LANES

210 Oak Grove Ave., South Beloit | 815-389-2238
bowlvikinglanes.com

For a more low-key bowling experience, Viking Lanes is the perfect place. The 24-lane bowling alley is open daily and offers bumper lanes and ball guides for kids. Viking Lanes also has Moonlight bowling where they turn the lights down, turn the music up, and add special effects lighting. They are also participants in the Kids Bowl Free program and offer kids' bowling leagues.

✓ *How to be a best mom:*

- **Sign up the kids to bowl all summer long at Park Lanes for free on the Kids Bowl Free website.**
- **Rent out the bowling alley for a fun all ages birthday party.**

Best Place to Ice-Skate

CARLSON ICE ARENA

4150 N Perryville Rd., Loves Park | 815-969-4069
icerockford.com/carlson

Glide into a day of fun at Carlson Ice Arena! Carlson Ice Arena features one large oval rink with bleacher seating for 600 spectators. The facility also houses Sapora Playworld, a three-story indoor playground for ages 12 and under. Carlson Ice Arena offers public skate on a regular basis with ice skates and hockey skates available for rent.

Besides skate rental, Carlson Ice Arena also offers protective gear such as helmets and pads for rent. Throughout the week, there are special offers on open skating. Other special events are held for holidays and days off of school. When kids need a break from skating, parents can head to the concession stand for drinks, food, and snacks. Vending machines are also available in the lobby.

Kids who are interested in becoming figure skaters or hockey players can take lessons at Carlson Ice Arena. Skate programs start as young as 18 months. Adults can also learn the fundamentals of skating. For those who would prefer to spectate, Carlson Ice Arena hosts a Spring Ice Show that showcases the best local talent and brings nationally recognized figure skaters to Rockford. Tickets are available to purchase for this show.

RIVERSIDE ICE ARENA

1151 W Locust St., Belvidere | 815-547-9557
belviderepark.org

If you want to ice-skate on an outdoor rink, Riverside Ice Arena is a great spot to go. They offer public skate, open hockey, and ice-skating lessons for all ages. Inside the Warming House, they rent skates and skate aids, and sell hot drinks. Riverside Ice Arena also hosts regular theme nights that include music, lights, and more. The rink is open throughout the winter, weather permitting.

How to be a best mom:

- **Check their Facebook page for announcements on theme nights like '90s night.**
- **Watch the Rockford IceHogs practice on the rink typically in November or December.**

STROLL ON STATE ICE SKATING

300 Elm St. | 815-968-5222
thebmocenter.com

During Stroll on State each November, families are invited to skate on the ice where the Rockford IceHogs play! This special event only happens once per year during the biggest holiday event in the Midwest. The BMO Center opens its doors to allow families to ice-skate on the Rockford IceHogs home ice. This event is free to attend each year and skates are limited and offered on a first-come, first-served basis.

How to be a best mom:

- **Head to the BMO Center during the Christmas tree lighting ceremony for a lighter crowd.**
- **Take a family photo in front of the Rockford sign in Davis Park.**

Best Place to Get Active

UW HEALTH SPORTS FACTORY

305 S Madison St. | 815-966-8770
uwhealthsportsfactory.com

Burn off some energy at UW Health Sports Factory's Open Gym! Located on the beautiful Rock River in downtown Rockford, the UW Health Sports Factory was once a vacant manufacturing building. This 108,000-square-foot building is now a premier indoor sports facility featuring eight full-size basketball courts, 16 volleyball courts, pickleball courts, a restaurant overlooking the water, five meeting spaces, and a 450-space parking lot. It is one of the largest sports facilities in the Midwest.

UW Sports Factory is a clean and spacious facility that offers daily open gyms. Drop-in sessions are available Monday through Friday—typically in the morning and early afternoon—for a minimal charge. A current schedule can be found on the UW Health Sports Factory website. Purchase a punch card for the year to take advantage of a discounted rate. Families can shoot hoops, throw discs, play some pickleball, spike volleyballs, or try their hand at table tennis.

The Courtside Grill located inside the facility serves delicious appetizers like cheese curds and dipping sauce, pretzel bites, and loaded fries as well as burgers, wings, veggie wraps, and pizzas. Make it a whole day with family game time followed by lunch or dinner and then a stop outside for a photo op at the Big Hoop!

YMCA OF ROCK RIVER VALLEY

200 Y Blvd. | 815-489-1252
rockriverymca.org

The YMCA of Rock River Valley keeps kids healthy and active all year round. They have three locations in the greater Rockford area to serve the community. Kids can take lessons in numerous sports including tumbling, dance, football, swimming, basketball, soccer, and more. Classes begin at 18 months old and continue through age 10. Kids can also enjoy Parents Night Out, which includes swimming, a movie, crafts, and games. Becoming a Y member allows parents to drop off kids ages infant through 12 for up to two hours of care while parents exercise or take classes at the Y.

✓ *How to be a best mom:*

- **Save the date for the YMCA's huge annual Easter egg hunt and Easter Bunny meet and greet.**
- **Join the Y and get to swim for free in public Rockford pools all summer!**

VICTORY PICKLEBALL

7003 N Alpine Rd., Loves Park | 815-846-3043
victorypb.com

Pickleball is sweeping the nation and Rockford has jumped on board. Victory Pickleball is the area's first indoor pickleball facility. They have 15 courts and an on-site kitchen serving classic grill food like burgers, wraps, and pizza. Victory Pickleball is a membership-only facility, but they offer a free bronze membership option. They also offer lessons for both kids and adults on how to play pickleball and improve your game.

✓ *How to be a best mom:*

- **Sign your kids up for a pickleball lesson so they can learn the trendy sport.**
- **Try your pickleball skills outside at the courts at Sinnissippi Park.**

Best Place to Practice Your Swing

PRAIRIEFIRE GOLF AND GRILL

6734 N German Church Rd., Byron | 815-234-3473
prairiefiregolf.com

Hit 'em straight and far at PrairieFire Golf and Grill! This year-round driving range that's fun for the whole family. PrairieFire gives golfers of all ages a chance to practice and improve their skills. PrairieFire uses Toptracer technology, which gives the golfer instant feedback, shot replays, and data on their shots.

Kids ages 8 and up will enjoy golfing, but this is an especially great place to spend quality time with teens. Families can bring their own golf clubs or use on-site rentals. After getting set up in a bay, families can choose which game they'll play on the Toptracer, a large screen display that offers a suite of modes for all skill levels. After hitting, Toptracer tells golfers their ball's speed, path, and more. There are six games, including Long Drive Competitions and Closest to the Pin.

Kids will love Go Fish, where golfers catch virtual fish and earn points. The "help shot" option allows kids to catch fish even if the Toptracer sensor doesn't sense their hit. PrairieFire also offers a delicious menu of appetizers and entrées that are brought to the bay. The menu includes chicken tenders, cheese curds, fried pickles, and more. Bays can be rented per hour so families can choose how long they stay.

GOLF SHACK'S DRIVING RANGE

1631 N Bell School Rd. | 815-397-3709
golfshack.com

Families can practice hitting golf balls at Golf Shack's driving range throughout the year. Golf Shack is open daily and has 40 grass and mat hitting bays. Each of these bays is covered to protect golfers from the rain and sun, but they are in the open air so dress accordingly. There are ball dispensers where you can get 42 or 84 balls to drive into the range. Golf Shack sells all of the golfing equipment you need to play including clubs, footwear, balls, tees, and more.

✓ *How to be a best mom:*

- **Don't forget to get something to eat, the Golf Shack is attached to Garrett's, a great place for food for the whole family.**
- **Make it a friendly competition to see which member of the family can drive the ball the farthest.**

INDOOR SPORTS CENTER

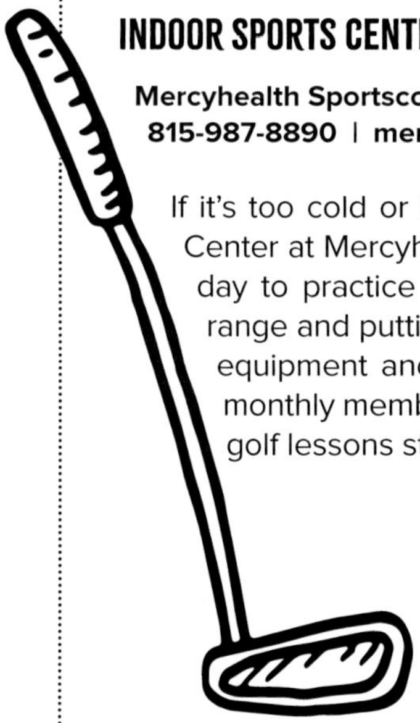

Mercyhealth Sportscore Two | 8800 E Riverside Blvd., Loves Park
815-987-8890 | mercyhealthsportscore.com/sportscore-two

If it's too cold or too hot to golf outside, head to the Indoor Sports Center at Mercyhealth Sportscore Two where it's always the perfect day to practice your swing. The indoor center includes a driving range and putting greens. All ages are welcome to bring their own equipment and practice. Families can buy buckets of balls or a monthly membership. The Indoor Sports Center also offers indoor golf lessons starting at age 4 through adults.

✓ *How to be a best mom:*

- **Sign the kids up for golf lessons indoors during the winter or wait until spring and summer to sign up for the Rockford Park District's outdoor lessons.**
- **Try your new golf skills at the family-friendly nine-hole course in Sinnissippi Park.**

Best Place to Hop into Easter

CHERRYVALE MALL

7200 Harrison Ave., Ste. 5
815-332-2440
shopcherryvalemall.com

Get a photo with the bunny and find some eggs! Easter isn't complete without photos with the Easter Bunny and egg hunts throughout the city. The Easter Bunny can be found at several places in Rockford, but the easiest spot to go to get a picture in the weeks leading up to Easter is at the CherryVale Mall. The Easter Bunny makes center court his temporary home for several weeks at the end of March through early April each year.

CherryVale Mall's Easter Bunny is a classic white bunny with pink ears and nose. The bunny is available on select days for photos in the center court. The center court is decorated for Easter with a wooden bench where the Easter Bunny and kids can take a photo together. Though visiting the Easter Bunny is free, no personal cameras or cell phones are allowed to take a photo with him. You will need to purchase a photo package in order to have your kids' photos taken.

The mall also offers select times to bring your family pet to get their photo taken with the Easter Bunny. You can reserve your spot to see the bunny on CherryVale Mall's website or you can show up and wait in line when the bunny is there. Please note, wait times may be higher in the days before Easter.

CAMP WINNEBAGO

5804 N Main St. | 815-489-3374
rockriverymca.org/locations/camp

Getting prizes, searching for eggs, and having fun are the three best parts of any Easter egg hunt. One of the best egg hunts is held annually at Camp Winnebago. The entire event is held outdoors on the grounds of camp. Kids are encouraged to bring their own Easter basket or bags to collect the thousands of eggs around the grounds. There are several golden eggs hidden that are redeemable for a special prize. The egg hunt is divided into age groups so kids can hunt with their peers. This event is always free to attend.

How to be a best mom:

- **Keep an eye out for other fun outdoor events throughout the year at Camp Winnebago including summer camp and a fall festival.**
- **Enjoy a walk on the trails at Camp Winnebago after the egg hunt.**

PECATONICA HIGH SCHOOL

1300 Main St., Pecatonica | 815-239-2611
pecschools.com

Pecatonica is a small town that knows how to throw a big egg hunt! Each year, the Community Easter Egg Hunt happens at Pecatonica High School in early April. The event includes more than 6,000 eggs that kids can run through the fields grabbing. These eggs are filled with candy and prizes. The event also includes an appearance from the Easter Bunny, bounce houses, a petting zoo, temporary tattoos, a Chuck a Duck tractor, a basketball game, and lots more. This event is always free to attend.

How to be a best mom:

- **Stop by The Third Street Station for an ice cream treat.**
- **Enjoy the beautiful spring weather by stopping by Blassingham Park's playground.**

Best Place to Watch a Performance

CORONADO PERFORMING ARTS CENTER

314 N Main St. | 815-968-5222
coronadopac.org

See a show at the historic Coronado! The Coronado Performing Arts Center has been a staple of downtown Rockford since 1927. The building was completely restored from 1999 through 2001 to showcase its beautiful interior. The theater holds 2,310 people and includes main floor and balcony seating.

Families will be dazzled by the beautiful architecture and timeless design of the theater. Marble and gold interlay decorate the walls, and a large staircase leads up to the balcony level. The theater has painted ceilings depicting a starry night sky. Gorgeous heavy red curtains conceal the stage from view until the show begins. All the floor seats feel close to the stage due to the theater's size. The Coronado Performing Arts Center hosts family-friendly events throughout the year.

In the past, the Coronado has welcomed such acts as Disney Jr., Bluey, Bubble Guppies, and many others, and Christmas productions such as *The Nutcracker* and *A Christmas Carol*. The Coronado is also home to the Rockford Symphony Orchestra. The venue is easy to navigate with bathrooms on the lower floor and a concession stand on the main level. There is a stunning marquee outside that makes for the perfect photo opportunity. A public parking garage is located across the street on North Main. Check their website to see upcoming kid-friendly shows.

BMO CENTER

300 Elm St. | 815-968-5222
thebmocenter.com

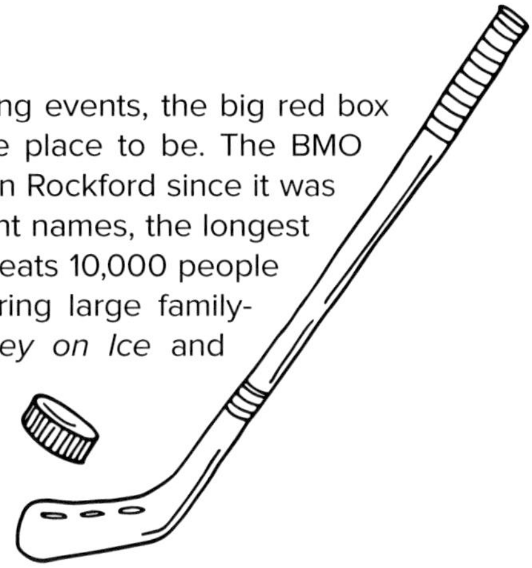

For bigger shows, rock concerts, and sporting events, the big red box otherwise known as the BMO Center is the place to be. The BMO Center has been a staple for entertainment in Rockford since it was built in 1981. It's also gone by several different names, the longest running being the Metrocentre. The facility seats 10,000 people in stadium-style fold-down seating. They bring large family-friendly shows to the area including *Disney on Ice* and *Monster Jam*. It is also where the Rockford IceHogs play all of their home games.

✓ *How to be a best mom:*

- **Save a couple bucks on tickets by buying them directly from the BMO Center box office which is open daily.**
- **Check out the IceHogs promotional schedule for fun events like Teddy Bear Toss and giveaways.**

SINNISSIPPI PARK MUSIC SHELL

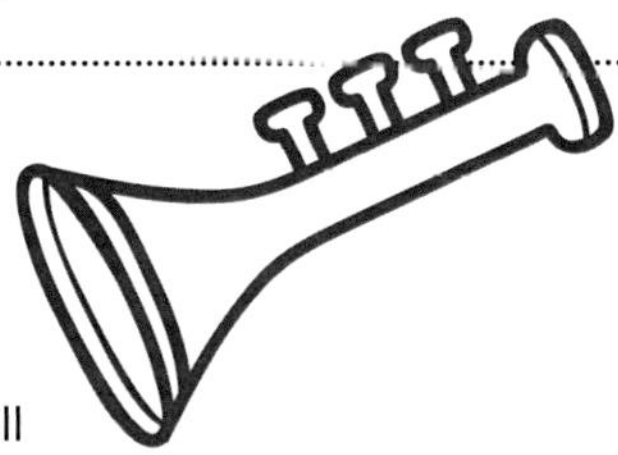

1401 N 2nd St. | 815-987-8858
rockfordparkdistrict.org/musicshell

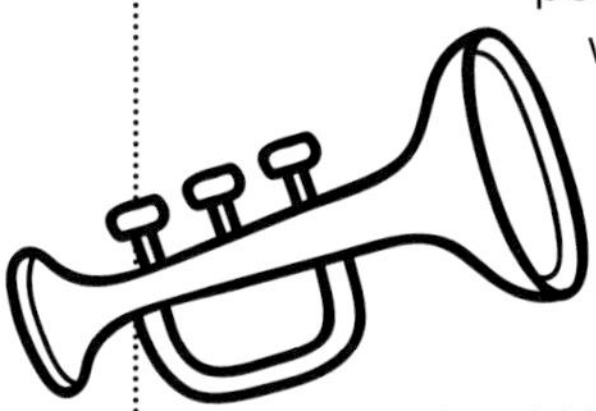

During the summer, Sinnissippi Park Music Shell offers free and low-cost outdoor concerts that are perfect for the whole family. The Sinnissippi Park Music Shell was built in 1950 to blend in with the beautiful tree-filled surroundings. The acoustic amphitheater can seat 700 on the permanent benches and up to 3,000 on the surrounding grass. There's nothing like listening to live music outdoors on a beautiful summer evening. Attending a concert at the Sinnissippi Park Music Shell should be on everyone's summer bucket list!

✓ *How to be a best mom:*

- **Walk to one of the two playgrounds in Sinnissippi Park to play before the show starts.**
- **Arrive early to get a good spot on the built-in benches.**

Best Place to Pick Up a Book

ROCKFORD PUBLIC LIBRARY

www.rockfordpubliclibrary.org

Find your next favorite book at Rockford Public Library! With three locations throughout the city, the Rockford Public Library is the largest library system in the greater Rockford area. Each location has unique attractions, but all three offer year-round children's programming.

At the time of this publication, Rockford Public Library will soon open their brand-new three-story riverfront main branch. The branch will include 50-foot windows, a massive children's section, space for teens, and multipurpose rooms. The second location is on Winnebago Street, where a beautiful building holds children's events. The third location is in East State Street's shopping corridor in a former Barnes & Noble. This location has a teen area with laptops to check out, video games, and a large book collection.

All three locations offer year-round, free to attend, weekly events geared toward kids. These events include story times, playgroups for young children, and events for kids of all ages. Previously, they've hosted American Girl tea parties, comic book creation events, and more. In the summer and winter, kids are encouraged to sign up for reading clubs, which reward time spent reading with giveaways and prizes. The library is open to all to visit and spend time in, but to borrow books you must be a Rockford resident or use a reciprocal card from a neighboring district. If you are not a resident, you can purchase a year-long membership.

MAZE BOOKS

406 E State St. | 779-970-5912
maze-books.com

If you want a book to keep as your own, Maze Books is a cozy gathering place for the community that sells a variety of new and used books including kids' books. In 2023, they moved into a bigger space downtown that holds events like author readings and chess clubs. Both parents and kids alike are sure to find something delightful to read at this locally owned shop.

How to be a best mom:

- **Mark your calendar for the annual indie book store crawl in February and visit all five independent bookstores in Rockford.**
- **Head to Wired Café or Inzombia Coffee afterward to get a pick-me-up.**

INKWELL BOOKS & THREADS

106A W Main St., Rockton | 815-957-0105
inkwellbooks.store

A short drive to Rockton brings you to Inkwell Books & Threads where you'll find the cutest little bookshop in the area. Inkwell is an independent bookstore that sells books of all genres including popular fiction. They have an entire children's section with books for kids of all ages including many picture books. In addition, they host regular events and book clubs and sell vintage clothing and reader-themed gifts.

How to be a best mom:

- **Make it a day of shopping by visiting nearby children's boutique Taylor + Max.**
- **Grab a coffee, smoothie, and baked good at DeeDee's and relax in the cozy atmosphere.**

Best Place to See Public Art

ROCKFORD PUBLIC ART TRAIL

gorockford.com/things-to-do/public-art-trail

Snap share-worthy pics at more than 100 stops on Rockford's Public Art Trail! Rockford has burst into color with the addition of more than 50 murals since 2019. Cre8IV (pronounced *Creative*) brought together talented artists to add life and vibrancy to empty walls and utility boxes throughout Rockford. Each spring and summer, artists are invited back to create more murals. Artwork is located throughout the greater Rockford area.

The murals celebrate Rockford through showcasing famous Rockford-made products, like screws and sock monkeys, as well as notable Rockfordians and the sports teams that called the area home. Many of the murals also include depictions of local wildlife. The Rockford Area Convention & Visitors Bureau created a Public Art Trail passport that families can use to locate and learn more about the art. This passport can be accessed through their website. The passport offers directions to the art and the option for families to earn points when they visit the artwork. Points can be redeemed for merch from the visitors bureau.

The trail gives families a greater appreciation for the Rockford area and its talented artists. Most of the public art is within a five-mile radius and there is public parking located near most of the pieces. More information about current Rockford Public Art Trail promotions can be found at gorockford.com.

DOWNTOWN BELVIDERE

Boone County Arts Council | 920 W Lincoln Ave., Belvidere
815-544-6242 | boonecountyarts.com

For even more public art, head to Belvidere, also known as the City of Murals. Belvidere received this distinction in 1997 after the first 10 murals were painted downtown. Belvidere has a variety of amazing Americana murals including an Eagle on VFW Post 1461, Art on the Lawn at 215 S State St., and Belvidere Seed Company at Buchanan and State Streets. They also have a variety of sculptures in Baltic Mill and throughout the city.

✓ *How to be a best mom:*

- **Add your own temporary art to downtown Belvidere at the annual Paint on State event held each June where kids can paint on the street.**
- **Grab a delicious breakfast at casual eatery, Farel's Grill.**

ROCKTON FOOD & SPIRITS

121 W Main St., Rockton | 815-624-5800
rocktonfoodspirits.gotoliquorstore.com

Head to downtown Rockton to see two more amazing murals! Rockton Food & Spirits has a beautiful mural of sunflowers on the side of the building painted by Lisa and Libbie Frost. These colorful blooms make for a great backdrop for a cute photo of your kid! A short walk from the first mural at 122 S Prairie St. is the second; this one is a colorful depiction of American white pelicans, which are the star of Rockton's annual Pelican Fest.

✓ *How to be a best mom:*

- **Head to Rockton in May to celebrate the annual Pelican Festival where the village welcomes the return of the American White Pelican to nearby Nygren Wetland Preserve.**
- **Check out the murals in the snow during Yeti Fest held in February each year.**

Best Place to Celebrate the Rockford Peaches

BEYER PEACHES STADIUM

245 15th Ave.

Take a tour of Rockford and learn more about the famous Rockford Peaches! Rockford was the home of the All-American Girls Professional Baseball League's Rockford Peaches from 1943 through 1954. The Rockford Peaches were the inspiration for the 1992 movie *A League of Their Own* starring Tom Hanks and Geena Davis. The Rockford Peaches have been a source of pride for the Rockford community for over 80 years. The Rockford Area Convention & Visitors Bureau launched gorockfordpeaches.com to provide information and ways Rockford celebrates their legacy.

The Rockford Peaches played at Beyer Stadium on the south side of Rockford during the 1940s and '50s. Today, families can stroll around the diamond, take a photo beneath the gatehouse and Rockford Peaches sign, and sit in the dugouts where there are pictures of the players displayed. Reenactments of games occasionally happen at Beyer Stadium.

Midway Village Museum is the best place to learn about the history of the Rockford Peaches. The *Girls of Summer* exhibit, dedicated to the history of the Rockford Peaches and their 12-year run, features memorabilia including uniforms, trophies, and photos. You can also head to midtown Rockford at 206 Seventh St. to see the Rockford Peaches' mural, featuring several Peaches players in action.

ROCKFORD ART DELI

402 E State St. | 312-725-4723
rockfordartdeli.com

Rockford Art Deli is a print shop located in downtown Rockford that celebrates all things Rockfordian, especially the famous Rockford Peaches. RAD is the best place to get Rockford Peaches gear such as hats, stickers, T-shirts, and hoodies. They have a variety of designs available including both text designs and graphics. They also have a shirt that celebrates *A League of Their Own* with the classic line "There's no crying in baseball." Rockford Peaches gear is available in onesies through adult sizes so the whole family can get decked out.

✓ *How to be a best mom:*

- **Check Rockford Art Deli's Facebook page for upcoming free print days where families can bring their own cotton shirts to be printed with a seasonal limited edition design for free.**
- **Pick up a unique local gift or gift card for someone who loves Rockford at RAD.**

PRAIRIE ST. BREWING CO.

200 Prairie St. | 815-277-9427
psbrewingco.com

Peaches fans can enjoy dinner in downtown Rockford at Prairie St. Brewing Co. This restaurant and brewery was built in 1957, and is the oldest brewery in Illinois. From 1945 to 1999 the building was used as a warehouse before being renovated and becoming a brewery again. The restaurant is in a beautiful location right off the Rock River with dockside dining available in the summer. They offer a peach wheat beer that parents can enjoy in honor of the legendary Peaches!

✓ *How to be a best mom:*

- **Visit Prairie Street Brewing Company in the summer months to eat dinner on the dock and enjoy live music during your meal.**
- **Save the date for holiday shopping and head to Prairie Street in December for their annual Handmade Market, a large vendor fair with artists selling unique gifts.**

Best Place to Try BMX

ROCKFORD BMX TRACK

4950 Safford Rd. | 815-874-8719
rockfordbmx.com

Kick up some dirt at the Rockford BMX Track! Located in Searls Park, Rockford BMX was started in 1977 by the Jaycee family for public BMX practice and racing. The highly ranked outdoor track has a covered staging area to make the rider's wait more comfortable. The track is nationally famous with riders flying in from all over the world for tournaments. BMX is a sport for all ages, with riders from 3 years to over 60.

Kids who want to learn can sign up for the Beginners League designed for newcomers. The four-session program teaches the skills to become race ready, with bike and helmet provided. Rockford BMX's coaches have decades of experience to help kids learn how to Race the Rock.

Once trained, they can join the USA BMX and participate in races. Practices and racing happen from April through October. Competitions include the Midwest Nationals, State Qualifier, and Race to 8 Finale. Rockford BMX often hosts the USA BMX Midwest Nationals, which brings over 5,000 riders and spectators to Rockford. Competitions are held in summer and allow spectators.

Rockford BMX holds a free open house on the first Saturday of each month during their season where kids can try a BMX bike and helmet for free. They also host a Ladies Only event for girls of all ages to try BMXing in a low-stress environment each August.

SUBVERSIVE CYCLING COMPANY

327 W Jefferson St. #1 | 815-708-7399
subversivecycling-company.shoplightspeed.com

Subversive Cycling Company not only sells BMX bikes, but they are also owned by a BMX rider! The shop focuses on providing the local cycling community with a family-friendly and inclusive atmosphere for riders from beginner to advanced. The shop is Rockford's premier place for Surly and All-City cycles and has a variety of bikes from fat bikes, mountain bikes, and road bikes. Subversive will get your kids set up on the right bike for their needs and skill level.

✓ *How to be a best mom:*

- **Call Subversive to make an appointment to take a test ride on a bike before you buy.**
- **If you already own a bike and need it tuned up or repaired, bring it to Subversive for all your bike care needs.**

KEGEL'S BICYCLE STORE

2605 Charles St. | 815-229-5826
kegelsbikes.com

When looking for a BMX bike, support local in the Rockford area! Kegel's Bicycle Store has been operating on Charles Street since 1975 though the business began in 1953 in downtown Rockford. Kegel's offers a variety of kids' bikes and BMX bikes for kids, teens, and adults. Bikes start at $400 and bike experts at the shop can make sure your kid finds the perfect bike for them.

✓ *How to be a best mom:*

- **Want something special? Kegel's can help you build a custom bike for BMX racing.**
- **Grab some cute bike 815 merch like hoodies and t-shirts for the biker in your life at Kegel's.**

Best Place to Roam a Farmers Market

ROCKFORD CITY MARKET

116 N Madison St., Ste. 207 | 815-977-5125
rockfordcitymarket.com

Experience a taste of Rockford at Rockford City Market! Created in 2010, Rockford City Market offers downtown Rockford a new farmers market experience. Rockford City Market harnessed the energy and excitement of downtown Rockford and combined it with a festival. The market has expanded from a few booths to an outdoor pavilion with more than 70 vendors and a live stage. Rockford City Market restored a space on Madison Street that housed the first locations of Velvet Robot and Crust and Crumble, among others. Rockford City Market runs May through September yearly.

Rockford City Market is where families can spend hours walking around the pavilion shopping, eating, and enjoying live music. Families can sample and purchase from some of the best local growers, artists, and bakers in Rockford. Two breweries are on-site, along with a Main Stage for local musicians and an Acoustic Stage. Each week there are food trucks that serve Korean, Mexican, Southern, and other dishes. Families can enjoy dinner and dessert, including churros, ice cream, and more. Admission is free.

Kids can enjoy street hockey, football, and basketball provided by the Rockford Park District. Families can take a free trolley ride during the market. The trolley follows the Rock River Recreation Path from the Outdoor Pavilion past Nicholas Conservatory before stopping at the *Symbol* and returning to the market.

NORTH END CITY MARKET

corner of N Main and Auburn Streets
rockfordcitymarket.com/northend

If Saturday morning farmers markets are more your speed, grab a cup of coffee and head to the North End of Rockford for the North End Market. It's a cute and quaint farmers market held on Saturday mornings from May through October at the corner of North Main and Auburn Road. Shop from local vendors selling fresh vegetables and fruit, honey, barbecue, baked goods, and handmade items. While you're there, make a stop at the Norwegian for some delicious brunch.

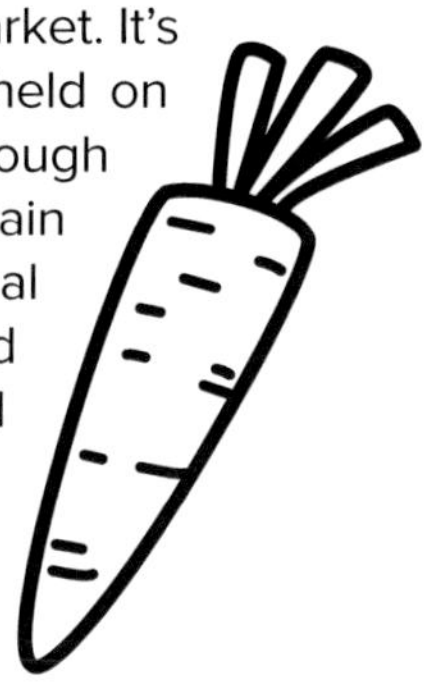

How to be a best mom:

- **Bring along the family dog, they are welcome at North End City Market!**
- **Try some local honey as well as fruits and veggies from farmers.**

EDGEBROOK FARMERS MARKET

1639 N Alpine Rd. | 815-226-0212
edgebrookshops.com/events/farmers-market

Make the midweek special by stopping at Edgebrook Farmers Market on Wednesday mornings from May through October. Edgebrook Farmers Market is a low-key and relaxed place to grab a coffee and walk around with the kids. You can find local farmers selling high-quality vegetables, fruits, flowers, plants, baked goods, honey, eggs, and more. If you want to stay for lunch, Baker Street Burgers is one of the best places in Rockford for a burger and fries.

How to be a best mom:

- **Be sure to stop and watch the local musicians performing at each market.**
- **Save the date for June when Edgebrook holds its annual Artsy Arts and Crafts fair.**

Best Place to Find Food on Wheels

NICHOLAS CONSERVATORY & GARDENS

1354 N 2nd St. | 815-987-8858
nicholasconservatory.com/food-truck-tuesdays

Sample some of the best and most unique cuisines in Rockford to go! Food Truck Tuesdays take place at Nicholas Conservatory & Gardens and the Rock River Recreation Path. The event began with only five food trucks in the driveway of Nicholas Conservatory; today more than 15 food trucks participate.

Food Truck Tuesdays runs weekly from May through October. The food trucks represent cultural cuisines including Mexican, Korean, Puerto Rican, Jamaican, and more. Trucks serve up dinner options like pulled pork barbecue sandwiches, garlic caramel chicken on a bao bun, wood-fired pizza, and more. After dinner, enjoy an Oreo-stuffed churro or homemade strawberry ice cream. Most of the food trucks take debit or credit, but bring cash just in case!

Forget about cooking on Tuesday night and head to the Rock River Recreation Path to try something new. Families can eat alongside a beautiful view of the Rock River. There's something for everyone with appetizers, entrées, desserts, and specialty drinks available. Trucks park in clusters so it's easy to visit several. Take little ones over to the Sinnissippi Exploration Station, close to the *Symbol*, to burn off some energy at the toddler playground. Families with older kids can take a stroll down the Rock River Recreation Path and enjoy some fresh air and public art.

SIZZ N FIZZ

200 Prairie St.
sizznfizz.com

Want a delicious smashburger to go? Sizz n Fizz offers a fantastic smashed burger with sizzy sauce on a Hawaiian bun as well as chicken nuggz, waffle fries, and cheese curds. They also offer plant-based options for those who want the taste without the meat. The fizz comes in with their selection of Wild Bill's soda in flavors like Rocket Pop and Cola. Kids and parents will love these burgers and fries. Sizz n Fizz is in different locations throughout the year but can often be found in the Kohl's parking lot.

How to be a best mom:

- **Bring your food to nearby Schoonmaker Park for a outdoor picnic.**
- **Try the Fizz sauce, it's delicious!**

CHEEZY'S GRILLED CHEESES

2842 11th St. | 815-310-0777
cheezysgrilledcheeses.com

Kids want grilled cheese, but parents want something a little fancier? Get both at Cheezy's Grilled Cheeses. Cheezy's offers a unique twist on classic grilled cheese sandwiches and melts. They offer eight weekly options to choose from. Kids can enjoy a classic grilled cheese with American cheese while parents can try a BBQ Bacon Smash or one of the other tasty combinations. Cheezy's is all over Rockford but can often be found at BJ's Place.

How to be a best mom:

- **Save yourself the trip and get Cheezy's Doordashed to your house.**
- **Take your Cheezy's to go and enjoy it at nearby Ken-Rock Park which has a playground.**

Best Place to See a Ski Show

SKI BRONCS WATER SKI SHOW

235 Evelyn Ave., Loves Park
skibroncs.com

Be awed and amazed at the Ski Broncs Water Ski Show! The Ski Broncs are a water-skiing team of young adults who audition each year to participate in the show. The Ski Broncs have performed at Shorewood Park for nearly 60 years. Each year, the Ski Broncs shows have different themes, like *Scooby Doo*, *The Flintstones*, and *Bill and Ted's Excellent Adventure*.

The Ski Broncs shows are free to attend, though they appreciate donations to help keep the tradition alive. The shows are about an hour long and are performed in the Rock River directly in front of Shorewood Park. Watching the Ski Broncs perform daring stunts while water-skiing is captivating. These tricks, including human pyramids, one-foot skiing, and more, can sometimes lead to wipeouts. The Ski Broncs aren't just performers; they're competitors. Throughout the season, they travel for competitions.

Shows happen on Wednesday and Friday evenings from the spring through early fall. Recent renovations to Shorewood Park have made it a fun destination to play before or after the shows. Concessions are available for purchase during the show. Bring bug spray to avoid mosquitos near the riverbank. After watching the show, head over to 5727 N 2nd St. to see the vibrant mural honoring the Ski Broncs.

ROCK AQUA JAYS SKI SHOW

Traxler Park | 600 N Main St., Janesville, WI
rockaquajays.com

Watch a team make magic on the water during the summer months by heading to Traxler Park in Janesville. The Rock Aqua Jays are 22 time National Champions who bring passion and creativity to the Rock River from Memorial Day through Labor Day each year. The team of talented youth performs a free show every Wednesday and Sunday. Expect to see amazing stunts like five-tier human pyramids as well as one-handed skiing and tricks. The team won a Guinness World Record in 2021 for performing eight barefoot pyramids held over 200 feet.

How to be a best mom:

- **Bring your own chair and blanket for chilly nights!**
- **Bring cash for the concession stand.`**

LEARN TO SKI CLINICS

235 Evelyn Ave., Loves Park
skibroncs.com

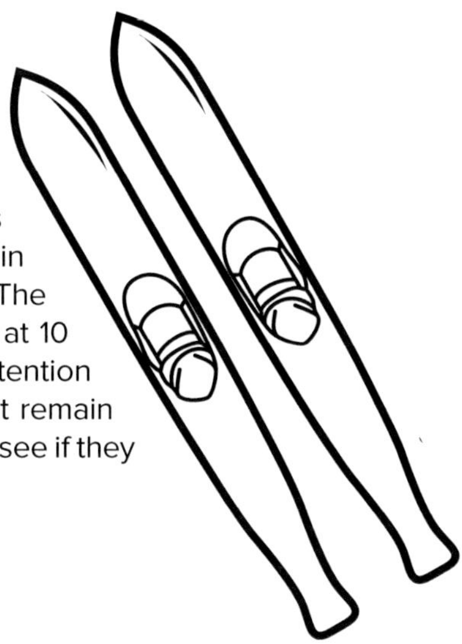

If your kids are inspired by the show and want to try the sport, the Ski Broncs offers Learn to Ski clinics at Shorewood Park several times each summer. These clinics allow kids to get in the water and learn how to stand on water skis. The clinics are two hours each. Clinics are capped at 10 kids or less so each person can get individual attention and support. Kids under 10 must have a parent remain on-site for the clinic. These clinics allows kids to see if they have what it takes to become a Ski Broncs star!

How to be a best mom:

- **Be sure to catch a free Ski Broncs show every Wednesday and Friday throughout the summer at Shorewood Park.**
- **Sign the kids up for swimming lessons through the Rock River Valley YMCA, Dolphin Swim Club, or Catch the Wave.**

Best Place to See a Summer Concert

SOUNDS OF SUMMER

Sinnissippi Park | 1401 N 2nd St. | 815-987-8858
rockfordparkdistrict.org/soundsofsummer

Groove and sway in the heart of Rockford all summer long! Sounds of Summer is an annual concert series held at Sinnissippi Park. Free and low-cost concerts featuring popular musicians and acts are held in the open-air Music Shell. The Music Shell has seating for over 700 on benches and 3,000 on the terraces and lawn. Come early to secure a spot!

Concerts run from early June through late August and are held outdoors, weather permitting. Most concerts are on Tuesdays and Thursdays and run two hours. Some concerts are premium and charge around $5 per person to attend. These concerts are typically bigger acts. Local talent also plays the Shell, with favorites including the Rockford Concert Band and Rock and Roll Institute. Several tribute bands play, including American English, a Beatles tribute band, and Blooze Brothers, a Blues Brothers tribute band.

Concessions including soft drinks, popcorn, and alcohol for those with ID are available. Families are also allowed to bring their own coolers and food, barring alcohol. Some premium shows include VIP seating for an additional cost. Each spring, the performer list is published for the summer's shows on Rockford Park District's website and social media pages. Premium show tickets can be purchased in advance. Free show seating is first come, first served. Bring water and bug spray when attending.

TUESDAY EVENING IN THE GARDENS

318 Spring Creek Rd. | 815-229-9390
andersongardens.org

Listening to music with the backdrop of a nationally recognized Japanese garden couldn't be any more peaceful! All summer long, Anderson Japanese Gardens holds concerts with both local musicians and Midwest acts. The concerts happen on the lawn and visitors need to bring their own chairs and blankets. Each concert is a few hours long. Concessions are available for purchase during the shows. Be sure to walk around the gardens while you're there.

✓ *How to be a best mom:*

- **Save the date for the annual Japanese Festival held each July where you can watch performances, shop, and learn about Japanese culture.**
- **Enjoy brunch in the beautiful Fresco that overlooks the gardens.**

WOODSON SUMMER SERIES

2715 S Main St. | 815-965-8146
klehm.org

Another beautiful outdoor concert venue in the summer is Klehm Arboretum. The Woodsong Summer Series offers concerts on the open lawn in the Fountain Garden. Attendees need to bring their own chairs and blankets. Families can bring in their own food and drink in coolers, barring alcohol. In previous years, there has also been ice cream for sale at the events. The concerts are geared toward all ages. Don't forget to bring swimsuits and towels to enjoy the kid's creek.

✓ *How to be a best mom:*

- **Take a picture with the purple dinosaur located in the Nancy Olson Children's Garden.**
- **Arrive early to get a good seat, they are first-come, first-served.**

Best Place to See a Movie under the Stars

FRIDAY NIGHT FLIX

Davis Park | 320 S Wyman St. | 815-968-5600
facebook.com/fridaynightflix

See a show under the stars at Friday Night Flix! Each summer, the City of Rockford hosts Friday Night Flix, three free movie nights downtown in Davis Park. These family-friendly events in June, July, and August typically run from 6 to 10 p.m. Admission is free, but other activities are offered for a small fee. Davis Park is undergoing redevelopment, which will add a skate park, splash pad, and play areas for more fun in upcoming years.

Friday Night Flix shows a popular kids' movie on a giant screen in the park—often a recent release, but sometimes a classic family movie like *Back to the Future*. Bring your own chairs and blankets since no seating is available in the park. Sunscreen and bug spray are good ideas, too. The movie starts when it gets dark, but there's a lot of fun happening before the show. Movie and cartoon characters walk around for meet and greets, and there are performers like magicians and balloon artists, bounce houses or obstacle courses, yard games provided by the Rockford Park District, and more.

Come hungry and dine from one of several food trucks on-site. Giveaways of popcorn or a drink are often offered for the first 500 people. Most of the vendors take credit or debit cards, but bring some cash just in case.

See a show under the stars in Davis Park!

NORTHEAST FAMILY YMCA

8451 Orth Rd., Loves Park | 815-885-6852
rockriverymca.org

Enjoy a movie under the stars from the YMCA of the Rock River Valley. During the summer at their Loves Park location, the Y shows family movies on a big inflatable screen outside. These movies are often popular hits from the past year or two. Not only can families enjoy a free movie outdoors, they can also indulge in some free fun with inflatables, activities, crafts, and sometimes appearances from the OSF Lifeline Helicopter. The events are moved indoors if the weather is bad.

How to be a best mom:

- **Bring your own blankets to get cozy outdoors, the temperature can get chilly!**
- **Be sure to take a picture with the characters and photo props.**

MCHENRY OUTDOOR THEATER

1510 Chapel Hill Rd., McHenry
goldenagecinemas.com

Take a drive to the McHenry Outdoor theater to enjoy an old-fashioned drive-in experience with modern amenities. Kids will love watching a movie from the car. Each showing includes two movies that run from approximately 9 p.m. to 1 a.m. There is also a concession stand on-site that sells full meals like burgers and fries, hot dogs, drinks, and more. Movies are shown daily. Families can bring lawn chairs and blankets or watch the movie from their car trunk or inside their cars.

How to be a best mom:

- **Check McHenry Outdoor Drive In's website for information on extended shows into December!**
- **Bring chairs and blankets to sit outside for the best view.**

Best Place to Be Dazzled by Local Talent

BENGT SJOSTROM THEATRE (STARLIGHT THEATRE)

Rock Valley College | 3301 N Mulford Rd. | 815-921-2160
rockvalleycollege.edu/community/starlight-theatre/index

Be amazed by local talent at Starlight Theatre! Opened in 2003, the 35,000-square-foot Bengt Sjostrom Theatre (Starlight Theatre) at Rock Valley College has a 200-foot retractable star-shaped roof, which allows audiences to see the night sky while being protected from the weather.

Every summer, Starlight Theatre puts on four shows for all ages and one Starlittle show. The shows vary each year and have included classics like *Cats, Chitty Chitty Bang Bang*, and *The Phantom of the Opera*; modern musicals like *Dreamgirls* and *In the Heights*; and others. Many of the shows are appropriate for all ages, though some are geared toward teens and older.

The Starlittle show is always performed in August and is geared toward a younger audience. These performances are held during select weekdays and one weekend. Starlittle shows have included *Madagascar, Pinkalicious*, and *The Stinky Cheese Man*. The shows are always upbeat, fun, and short, lasting 90 minutes or less so kids stay engaged. There's a concession stand selling drinks, popcorn, and themed treats during the shows.

The theater company also does a Shakespeare production each fall on the Starlight lawn. During the winter months, they put on a Tradition show that is often Christmas-themed. This show is performed in a temporary wooden cabin constructed around the stage and audience.

THE STUDIO ROCKFORD

7326 N Cherryvale Mall Dr. | 815-904-4253
thestudiorockford.com

If your kids would like to see their peers perform, the Studio puts on excellent musicals throughout the year at Rockford University's Maddox Theater. The talented kids and teens in these productions have performed musicals such as *Newsies, Tarzan, Descendants, The Wizard of Oz*, and more. The owners also wrote a wonderful original musical called *Girls of Summer* that celebrates the Rockford Peaches. Tickets can be purchased for any show on the Studio's website.

✓ *How to be a best mom:*

- **Register your talented kids to audition for an upcoming show!**
- **Stop by the concession stand and merch booth during the intermission.**

CYT CHICAGO ROCKFORD

718 Harlem Rd., Machesney Park
cytchicago.org/rockford

Kids can find their place on the stage at CYT Chicago Rockford. This youth theater group offers weekly classes during the school year on a variety of topics including drama, voice, and dance and presents a showcase at the end of each session. They also put on several performances per year including favorites like *Honk!, Lion King Jr.*, and *The Little Mermaid*. Shows are performed at the Hononegah High School Performing Arts Center and tickets can be purchased on the CYT Chicago Rockford website.

✓ *How to be a best mom:*

- **Sign your kids up for CYT Chicago Rockford programs where they can learn to act, sing, and dance on stage.**
- **Support local theater by checking out performances from your local middle school and high school throughout the school year.**

Best Place to Indulge in a Sweet Treat

ZAMMUTO'S

725 Kent St.
815-962-9180
zammutos.com

Do something different and try the Unusual at Zammuto's! Zammuto's has been serving up sweet treats and hot eats every spring through fall since 1925. Zammuto's is best known for their original granita. This Italian sweet treat, which originated in Sicily, is a simple, shaved-ice dessert made from sugar, water, and flavoring. Zammuto's offers 13 flavors, including cherry, blue raspberry, lemon, mango, peach, and passion fruit.

Zammuto's is open from late May through September. They offer a variety of desserts as well as hot food options—chicken wings, chili cheese dogs, hamburgers, and more—but their real draw is their sweet treats. Popular items include Oreo flurries, strawberry cheesecake sundaes, Twinkle cups, and root beer floats. Zammuto's has picnic bench seating available near their parking lot or treats can be taken to go.

Adventurous customers can give the Unusual a try! It's a combination of granita and soft-serve ice cream. The most popular flavor combination is the cherry granita with lemon ice cream. With more than 400 possible variations, families can create the combination they like best. Feeling fancy? Get Twinkles (sprinkles with crunchy bits) on the Unusual. Families with food sensitivities will appreciate that Zammuto's ice cream is both lactose free and gluten free.

DAIRYHAUS

113 E Main St., Rockton | 815-624-6100
facebook.com/dairyhausrockton

Another place to get a sweet treat in the summer while supporting a local business is Dairyhaus in Rockton. This adorable brick building has been serving up homemade ice cream since 1983. Each batch of ice cream is handmade and the flavors rotate on a daily basis. Some of the most popular flavors include wedding cake, mint chip, and chocolate chip cookie dough. Don't skip out on the homemade waffle cones either! Locals can also find Dairyhaus ice cream at Schnucks.

✓ *How to be a best mom:*

- **Relax and enjoy the adorable outdoor seating next to Dairyhaus on a hot summer night.**
- **Bring your ice cream to the nearby Village Green Park and enjoy the playground.**

DAIRY DEPOT

5413 N 2nd St., Loves Park
facebook.com/dairydepotlovespark

Dairy Depot is another Rockford area staple that's been in business since 1984. This seasonal ice cream shop becomes a soup and bread shop called Mama's Feel Good Food during the winter months, but from Memorial Day to Labor Day, they are slinging soft-serve in the cow-print building. Dairy Depot offers vanilla or chocolate soft-serve ice cream with a variety of candy toppings and sundae options. They offer outdoor seating so families can enjoy their ice cream outside on a hot summer night. Try a banana split next time you're there!

✓ *How to be a best mom:*

- **During the fall and winter months, try the soup and bread shop, Mama's Feel Good Food, located in Dairy Depot.**
- **Try the flavor of the week which rotates all summer long!**

Best Child-Friendly Breakfast Spot

THE NORWEGIAN

1402 N Main St. | 815-329-6191
thenorwegian.com

Find eggs, bacon, and fun at these breakfast spots! It can be hard to find a great place to eat with kids, but the Norwegian delivers on both taste and atmosphere. The restaurant specializes in Norwegian fare, locally sourced ingredients, bespoke cocktails, and the most important meal of the day, breakfast!

The Norwegian's food is kid-friendly with American brunch items as well as Nordic specialties like gravlax and frikadeller. Ableskiver, or pancake balls, are one of the most popular options for kids. These delicious morsels come with maple syrup and house raspberry jam. They also offer other breakfast staples like omelets, shakshuka, fresh fruit, and mimosas. In the back of the restaurant, families can lounge on comfortable chairs placed near a fireplace. In the front area, long bench tables are perfect for kids, and high chairs are available.

The biggest perk of coming to the Norwegian for breakfast is their play area, which is flooded with light from the large windows. The play area includes a wall made of houses where imaginative play is encouraged. Bins are tucked away full of train tracks, blocks, and other small toys for kids to play with on the rug. The Norwegian also serves delicious dinners on weekends and hosts a family-friendly SnoMarket in December where they turn their back alley into a Nordic fishing village.

JOHNNY PAMCAKES

3700 E State St. | 815-229-7415
johnnypamcakes.com

Johnny Pamcakes is a spot where even the pickiest eater can find something to enjoy! Johnny Pamcakes is a locally owned business named after the owners, John and Pam. The restaurant has been in business for more than a decade and offers delicious breakfast favorites including skillets, buttermilk pancakes, french toast, and lunch options too. The kids' menu has silver-dollar pancakes, which are the perfect size for little ones, as well as kid favorites like peanut butter and jelly, grilled cheese, and chicken fingers. The atmosphere is cozy and diner-like and you'll feel right at home there.

✓ *How to be a best mom:*

- **If you're closer to Cherry Valley, check out Johnny Pamcakes second location in the Kegel Harley Davidson building.**
- **Enjoy pancakes for breakfast, lunch, or dinner, they are served all day!**

STOCKHOLM INN

2420 Charles St. | 815-397-3534
stockholminn.com

A Rockford staple, Stockholm Inn has been serving up breakfast Swedish style since 1968. They are best known for their world-famous Swedish pancakes, which are a delicious thinner style of pancake topped with powdered sugar and lingonberry jam. They also serve up a variety of other breakfast foods including omelets, buttermilk pancakes, skillets, and fresh orange juice. Stockholm Inn is also open for lunch and dinner with their menus including both Swedish favorites and American staples. The atmosphere is comfortable, casual, and family-friendly.

✓ *How to be a best mom:*

- **Save the date to visit during the Christmas season and listening to strolling carolers while you eat.**
- **Try one of the daily specials or the world famous Swedish pancakes.**

Best Place for Treats and Snacks

LA MICHOACANA MEXICAN CREAMERY

1714 E Riverside Blvd., Loves Park | 815-977-5182
lamichoacanamexicancreamery.com

Feast on sweet treats and savory concoctions at locally owned ice creamery and snack shop La Michoacana Mexican Creamery. The family-owned business has been a part of Rockford since 2013 and has expanded to three area locations.

La Michoacana carefully curates authentic Mexican recipes, made in small batches with locally sourced ingredients whenever possible. For those with a sweet tooth, La Michoacana makes dozens of flavors of paletas (popsicles) in-house, including lime, strawberry, and bubble gum. They also serve homemade ice cream in flavors such as tres leches, Snickers, and guava. Try their churro sundae made with fresh churros, caramel, chocolate syrup, and ice cream. Fruit lovers will enjoy the Pina Loca, a pineapple filled with fruit and drizzled with chamoy, lime, and tajin.

For those who love something savory, La Michoacana serves walking tacos made with Doritos, hot sauce, sour cream, and ground beef or pork rinds. They also offer elotes (Mexican corn), Hot Cheetos with hot cheese, and Wagon Wheels. Drink lovers can get energy drinks mixed with chamoy and other flavorings, agua fresca, slushies, and more. They offer fresh flavors of horchata, chia lime, and creamy strawberry. La Michoacana has a seating area where families can enjoy their food and a photo op under their neon sign that declares "Ice cream makes me feliz."

LA MICHOACANA HOMEMADE ICE CREAM

3840 Broadway | 779-774-9553
facebook.com/lamichoacana

Located on the south side of Rockford, La Michoacana Homemade Ice Cream offers a delightful mix of Mexican culture and American favorites. They make their homemade ice cream in store with the best quality Wisconsin dairy. They offer 30 rotating flavors including tres leches, rice pudding, and more. They also offer snacks like flaming elotes (corn, mayonnaise, spices, and Hot Cheetos dust), churro bites, and traditional Mexican hot chocolate for warming up on cold days. They are open year-round.

✓ *How to be a best mom:*

- **Take your treats to go and head to Alpine Park where kids can enjoy the fantastic Paulyground playground.**
- **Try the churros bites with your choice of ice cream and toppings.**

LA MICHOACANA TROPICAL OASIS

530 Blackhawk Blvd., South Beloit | 779-475-2089
facebook.com/michoacanatropicaloasis

Head over to South Beloit for more delicious treats at La Michoacana Tropical Oasis. They are open seasonally from spring through late fall. They offer all the sweet treats you'd expect like ice cream, homemade popsicles, mangonadas, agua frescas, and fresh fruit. They also serve up savory snacks like elotes, chips with all the toppings, and chicharrones (pork rinds with toppings). They have lactose-free and vegan options available too.

✓ *How to be a best mom:*

- **Bring your ice cream to South Beloit City Park which has a playground, picnic tables, and Lake Victoria.**
- **Enjoy your ice cream or snack on their beautiful patio that's surrounded by plants and flowers.**

Best Place to Take a Dip

SAND PARK POOL

1401 E Riverside Blvd., Loves Park | 815-987-8806
rockfordparkdistrict.org/sandparkpool

Cool off on a hot day at Sand Park Pool! Sand Park Pool is the perfect place for the whole family to take a dip. The pool is completely fenced in and has lots of free parking.

Sand Park Pool includes several areas that are perfect for younger kids. Toddlers will love the large wading pool, which is roughly two feet deep. Parents can join their toddlers in the water or relax in lounge chairs under poolside umbrellas. Kids ages 2 to 8 will be thrilled with Penguin Pond, which includes a large play structure with spraying features and slides. There is also a mini body waterslide that's perfect for little kids. The ride is slow and smooth and ends in a two-feet-deep pool.

Sand Park Pool's main gem is the large L-shaped pool that ranges from three to five feet deep. This pool is great for lap swimming and doing cannonballs off the side. It has a diving well with two drop slides and a one-meter diving board. Kids should be strong swimmers before using the deep end. Sand Park Pool also has a concession stand that sells drinks, hot dogs, pizza, and ice cream. There are plenty of shaded picnic tables to enjoy a snack. A bathhouse with dressing rooms, showers, and changing tables is also available.

ALPINE POOL

4310 Newburg Rd. | 815-987-8804
rockfordparkdistrict.org/alpinepool

Alpine Pool is located in Alpine Park, which is also home to a fantastic playground. Alpine Pool is an L-shaped pool that ranges from three to 12 feet deep. The pool is not heated so it may be a little chilly at the beginning of the season. There is plenty of room for kids to splash and play in the pool. The pool's deep end has one diving board and two tube slides that kids ages 6 and up will love. There is also a wading pool for the youngest swimmers.

✓ *How to be a best mom:*

- **Bring a change of clothes to play at Paulyground in Alpine Park after you swim.**
- **Use your Rock River Valley YMCA membership to get in free all summer long.**

HARKINS AQUATIC CENTER

910 Acorn St. | 815-987-8805
rockfordparkdistrict.org/harkins-aquatic-center

Rockford's only free place to swim is Harkins Aquatic Center. Harkins includes a family pool with zero-depth entry that goes up to four feet deep. There is also a twisted waterslide that kids will love going on, and a children's spray pool. There are several umbrellas for shade and seating available around the pool. There is also a changing room, showers, and a concession stand on-site that sells food and drinks.

✓ *How to be a best mom:*

- **Throughout the week, Harkins offers free drop-in swim lessons. Check the Rockford Park District website for dates and times.**
- **Rent one of the Rockford area pools after hours for an unforgettable birthday party!**

Best Place to Have Fun in the Sun

HURRICANE HARBOR ROCKFORD

7820 Cherryvale N Blvd., Cherry Valley
sixflags.com/hurricaneharborrockford

Race down a waterslide at Rockford's outdoor water park! Hurricane Harbor Rockford is a 43-acre water park where families can spend the whole day having fun in the sun. The park is open Memorial Day weekend through Labor Day weekend. Hurricane Harbor offers both daily passes and season passes.

Hurricane Harbor has 12 slides, including the Tidal Wave, the Midwest's first tailspin waterslide. The Little Lagoon is the spot for babies and toddlers; there are cute animals to climb on, a shallow pool to splash in, and swings. Preschoolers through tweens will enjoy the Caribbean Cove, a huge playground with water features and a giant bucket that dumps 1,000 gallons of water every 10 minutes. Families will also enjoy floating down the lazy river and riding the waves in the gigantic Tsunami Bay wave pool. For bigger kids and adults, there are several thrill rides including the Riptide Rush, a seven-story body slide; several tube slides; and the Tidal Wave, which descends 43 feet and has colorful special effects.

Hurricane Harbor also offers several dining options for guests. Paradise Pizza serves up individual pizzas and garlic knots. The Surfside Kitchen makes hot dogs, burgers, and loaded fries. The Totally Kickin' Kitchen offers chicken strips and buffalo chicken sandwiches. Several concessions also offer ice cream, Dippin' Dots, and slushies.

SAND PARK POOL

1041 E Riverside Blvd., Loves Park | 815-987-8806
rockfordparkdistrict.org/sandparkpool

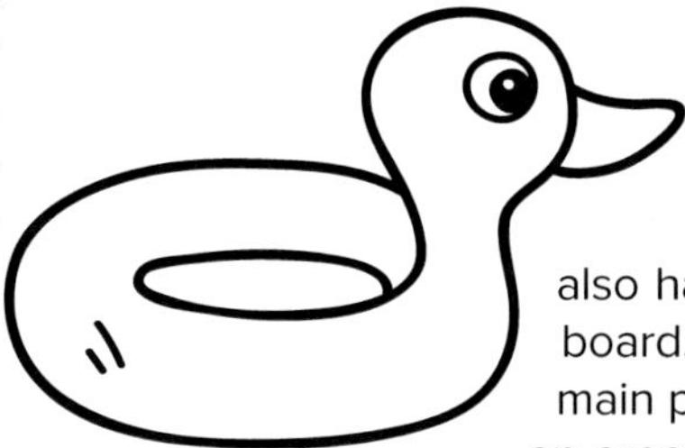

If you have kids under 5, Sand Park Pool is a great option for a day in the sun with less of a crowd. Sand Park Pool offers a full-size swimming pool that ranges from three feet to 12 feet deep. They also have a diving well with two tube slides and a diving board. A traditional wading pool can be found next to the main pool. Little kids will particularly love Penguin Pond—an area with a slow-moving waterslide and play structure, with spraying features, that resembles a smaller version of Caribbean Cove at Hurricane Harbor.

How to be a best mom:

- **Bring cash or your debit card for concessions at Sand Park Pool that include ice cream and hot food.**
- **If your kid has a summer birthday, have their party at Sand Park Pool for a great time.**

WOODSTOCK WATER WORKS

1313 Kishwaukee Valley Rd., Woodstock | 815-338-4363
woodstockrecreationdepartment.com/recreation/page/woodstock-water-works

Head to Woodstock for a day in the sun at Woodstock Water Works. This aquatic center includes attractions for the whole family. There is a zero-depth family pool with two big waterslides that kids must be 48 inches to ride. There are spray and play features in the shallow end of the family pool including a mushroom and small play structure with slide. There is also a sand pit with play equipment for kids to enjoy. Concessions are available on-site.

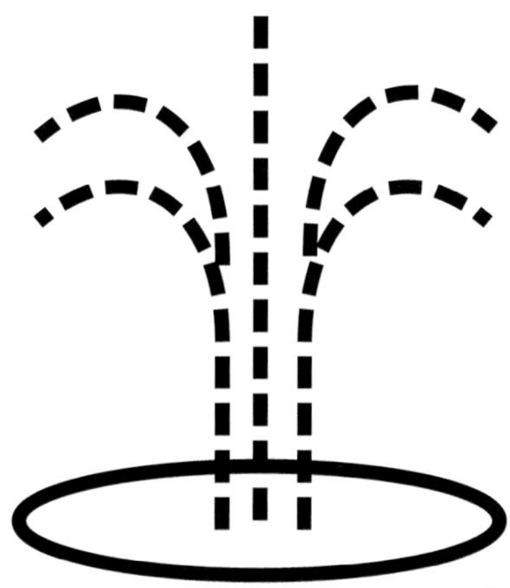

How to be a best mom:

- **Check Woodstock Water Works website for special events throughout the season including a duck drop.**
- **After a day at the pool, head to nearby Millie's Michoacana for a sweet treat.**

Best Place to Enjoy the Beach

PEARL LAKE

1220 Dearborn Ave., South Beloit | 815-389-1479
pearllakebeach.com

Dig your toes in the sand at Pearl Lake! Pearl Lake is a man-made lake that was originally a sand and gravel pit that supplied construction projects for decades. In the 1960s, a local family turned it into a recreation spot for camping, swimming, and scuba diving. It was a private RV park from 2019 to 2023, but a new owner has reopened the beach to the public.

Pearl Lake has a soft, sandy beach surrounding piercing blue waters. The water gradually reaches a depth of about 30 feet. Lifeguards are not present, and children under 16 must be accompanied by an adult. In 2023, Pearl Lake added a large inflatable floating obstacle course for kids to climb. An on-site bar and grill serves hot dogs, hamburgers, ice cream, and drinks, including beer and wine. Beachgoers can bring their own coolers, but no glass containers are permitted. Pearl Lake is a lively place on the weekends with music and food trucks on-site. For those who want to stay in the shade, beach pavilions are first come, first served, so get there early!

The lake is also a popular place for scuba divers. The water has excellent visibility for diving and some fun finds to explore underwater including a school bus, a small submarine, and a *Lady of the Lake* statue.

ROCK CUT STATE PARK

7223 W Lane Rd., Loves Park | 815-885-3311
dnr.illinois.gov/parks/park.rockcut.html

Want to build a sandcastle? Olson Beach located in Rock Cut State Park has sand galore on its swimming beach. The beach is surrounded by beautiful trees and grassy paths. Olson Lake is 60 acres and includes a swimming area and a launch for kayaks and paddleboats. The beach is open daily from May through September. There is also a concession stand on-site that sells ice cream, drinks, and snacks. Bring your sand toys to play!

How to be a best mom:

- **Get an ice cream cone at the concession stand and take a walk on the many wooded trails.**
- **Rent a water trike or peddle boat for more fun on the water.**

LAKE LOUISE

8840 N Rte. 2, Byron | 847-615-2013
lakelouiservresort.com

Another local beach has reopened to the public and is now a place where families can enjoy a day in the sand. Lake Louise offers a rustic lake experience with a large sandy beach. The lake has an inflatable floating obstacle course, which was added in 2022. Kids must wear a life jacket when enjoying the obstacle course. There is also a pool on-site. Families can buy day passes to visit the lake, which is open on weekends from Memorial Day through Labor Day. Lake Louise also offers both RV and tent camping in their campground.

How to be a best mom:

- **Bring a change of clothes to play on the playground after you swim.**
- **Make a whole weekend of it and go camping at the lake.**

Best Place to Tube Down the River

SUGAR RIVER ADVENTURES

Rockton | 815-629-2020
sugarriveradventures.com

Let the good times flow on the Sugar River! Sugar River Adventures offers a family-friendly tubing experience on the Sugar River. Families depart from the Colored Sands Forest Preserve in Rockton and float 1.5 miles to reach the Sugar River Forest Preserve. The average time for a float is 75 minutes, but families are welcome to spend as much time as they want on the river as long as they're off the water by 5 p.m.

Sugar River Adventures provides the tubes, which come in two sizes. Small kids can ride in their red tubes, which have closed bottoms. This allows kids to sit in the tube without touching the water. Bigger kids and adults ride in oversized blue tubes with open bottoms. Families get a cooler tube that can hold a dry bag, a cooler with drinks and snacks, and clothing. Tubes are secured together with bungee cords so members of the same party stick together as they float.

The best part of the float is arriving at the beach, which is a great place to enjoy a picnic and go swimming. Sugar River Adventures provides life jackets and encourages kids to wear them the whole time they are on the river. Bring a dry bag, water shoes, drinks, snacks, sunscreen, and some beach toys for the sand.

Float 1.5 miles to the Sugar River Forest Preserve!

WHITE PELICAN TUBING

201 N 2nd St., Oregon | 815-263-4088
whitepelican.biz

Head to Oregon, Illinois, to enjoy tubing down a calmer stretch of the Rock River. White Pelican offers tubing as well as other water sport rentals. They are open daily from April through Columbus Day, weather permitting. They offer self-guided trips down the Rock River for all ages. If you'd like a longer experience, they also offer overnight trips. Tubes for rental include individual tubes with a closed bottom, which are perfect for young kids, and two-person tubes with an open bottom. Tubing trips are offered from Castle Rock State Park and take two to four hours to complete.

✓ *How to be a best mom:*

- **Stop at Lowden State Park to see Black Hawk, the second largest concrete statue in the world.**
- **Head to Oregon Park West for an amazing nature-themed splash pad that's free to use.**

FOX HOLLOW RIVER TUBING

2480 N 41st Rd., Sheridan | 815-867-8823
foxhollowtubing.com

Can't get enough tubing? A short drive to Sheridan will take you to the longest float trip in the state. The Fox Hollow River Tubing adventure happens on the Fox River and lasts between three and eight hours. These adventures are offered daily from May through September, weather permitting. Kids ages 12 and under are required to wear life jackets. There is no age or weight limit to participate. They also offer shorter one- to three-hour trips.

✓ *How to be a best mom:*

- **Stay for the weekend at the family-friendly Fox River Resort at Sheridan where your family can enjoy an indoor waterpark.**
- **After a day on the river, stop by Chocolate Shoppe Ice Cream for a cone.**

Best Place for Water Sports

WEST ROCK WAKE PARK

1420 S Pierpont Ave. | 815-596-9025
westrockwakepark.com

Get soaked and try something new at West Rock Wake Park! West Rock Wake Park is a cable wakeboarding park located in Levings Park. Traditionally, wakeboarding requires a boat to pull the rider, but West Rock Wake Park's cable system moves the rider through the course and stops if they fall off their board.

West Rock offers beginner lessons, called their Never Ever class, where they make sure a person is able to stand on the wakeboard and be towed by the cable. Kids as young as 7 can try wakeboarding. Families can book all four spots of a Never Ever class to learn together. The next step is to take a Slow-Ride class, which is perfect for riders who can jump one wake, carve on their toes and heels, and ollie or surface 180. Once kids get comfortable on the slow ride, they can try the course, which has obstacles including kickers, ramps, and rails. The full-size cable allows kids to do grabs, flips, spins, and more.

In the summer, West Rock hosts summer camps for kids at different levels of wakeboarding. Parents can purchase a membership that allows kids to wakeboard during open hours throughout the week. The wake park has events throughout their season and often invites professional wakeboarders to teach a lesson or show off their skills.

The whole family can try cable wakeboarding lessons.

THE ROCK RIVER

313 N Madison St. | 815-636-9066
rocktownadventures.com

Want to try a variety of water sports? Rocktown Adventures has you covered! They rent kayaks, stand-up paddleboards, canoes, tandems, and fishing kayaks for a day of adventure on the Rock River. Rocktown Adventures not only offers rentals, but they also offer lessons for people of all ages to learn how to safely enjoy water sports. There are several paddle experiences available ranging from one hour to three hours. There are also lessons for beginners through intermediate on kayaking and paddleboarding. Life jackets must be worn at all times on a Rocktown rental.

✓ *How to be a best mom:*

- **Catch another amazing water race during the annual Anything That Floats race in August on the Rock River.**
- **If you'd rather view watersports, head to the Rock River in October to see the annual Regatta race.**

PIERCE LAKE

7223 W Lane Rd., Loves Park | 815-885-3311
dnr.illinois.gov/parks/park.rockcut.html

If you'd prefer to get out on a calmer body of water, head to Rock Cut State Park to enjoy the beautiful Pierce Lake. You'll get a close-up view of the water and the natural beauty of the state park surrounding it. Rocktown Adventures also operates the Outdoor Store, which offers a variety of rentals including kayaks, tandem kayaks (perfect for mom and me dates), canoes, pedal boats, stand-up paddleboards, and the super-fun water trikes. They are open from April to October each year. Rocktown Adventures also offers classes and introduction to water sports throughout the summer including the Kids on Water series geared toward kids ages 5 and up.

✓ *How to be a best mom:*

- **Enjoy a parent and me day on the water by renting a peddle boat or tandem kayak.**
- **Sign up siblings for Kids on Water so they can learn to kayak together.**

Best Way to Get Outdoors and Enjoy Nature

ROCKTOWN ADVENTURES

313 N Madison St.
815-636-9066
rocktownadventures.com

Get your kids outdoors, active, and on the water! Throughout the year, Rocktown Adventures offers ways for families to get out and enjoy the outdoors, no matter the season. Rocktown Adventures has two locations, one near the Rock River in downtown Rockford, and the second in Rock Cut State Park by Pierce Lake.

In the summer, they offer paddle-sport rentals including kayaks, stand-up paddleboards, tandem kayaks, canoes, pedal boats and more. They also offer lessons for both kids and adults on how to use these watercrafts safely. The Kids on Water class teaches kids ages 5 and up how to paddle a kayak and explore the lake. Parents do not have to paddle but must remain on-site during the class. In the winter, Rocktown Adventures offers snow-sports rentals so you can stay active and enjoy a winter wonderland. They rent cross-country skis, snowshoes, and roller skis and offer half price on all youth rentals (12 years old and under).

Families who want to try camping but don't want to invest in expensive equipment can rent everything they need for a weekend of camping from Rocktown Adventures. They rent tents for four to six people, sleeping bags, stoves, and cook sets for up to a week. They will also show you how to use the equipment before you go.

KISHWAUKEE GORGE NORTH

4643 Blackhawk Rd., Cherry Valley | 815-877-6100
winnebagoforest.org/items/kishwaukee-gorge-north

If you want to enjoy a hike in nature, head to Kishwaukee Gorge North for beautiful scenery including prairie land, ravines, and woods. There are nearly three miles of hiking trails including some grass and dirt paths. There are also man-made wooden steps along the side of the gorge, which opens up for a beautiful view of the Kishwaukee River. This is a great path to hike with kids!

✓ *How to be a best mom:*

- **Set a goal to visit all 44 forest preserves in Winnebago County during your kid's childhood.**
- **Grab some ice cream from Cattle and Cream in Cherry Valley after your hike.**

SEWARD BLUFFS

16999 Comly Rd., Seward | 815-877-6100
winnebagoforest.org/items/seward-bluffs

In the fall, Seward Bluffs is a gorgeous location to hike with your family. This nature preserve spans 400 acres and includes woods, streams, and dolomite cliffs. It is one of the most beautiful forest preserves in Winnebago County and a great place for family photos. The variety of scenery makes for a fun hike during any season, but October is the best time to see all of the leaves changing colors. During the summer, you can camp at the campgrounds in the preserve as well.

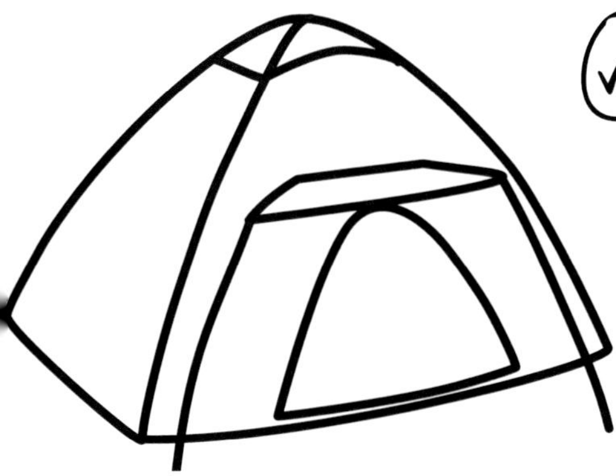

✓ *How to be a best mom:*

- **Get family photos taken in the spring, summer, or fall at this popular and gorgeous location.**
- **Head over to the playground after you enjoy a walk outdoors.**

Best Place to Go Fishing

FOUR LAKES FOREST PRESERVE

10207 Fish Hatchery Rd., Pecatonica
815-877-6100
winnebagoforest.org/items/four-lakes

Cast your line and see what nibbles at Four Lakes Forest Preserve! Located in Pecatonica, Four Lakes Forest Preserve is best known for its four small, man-made lakes that offer fishing. Expect to catch a variety of fish including bluegill, catfish, brown bullhead, redear sunfish, and northern pike. Families are welcome to keep and eat the fish they catch, except for largemouth bass, which are catch and release.

Four Lakes Forest Preserve spans 186 acres and has restrooms and drinking water available on-site. There is a shelter house and picnic tables for families to enjoy an outdoor meal, but the location does not have a playground. Fishing at any of the Winnebago County forest preserves requires a valid Illinois fishing license for ages 17 and up (available online through exploremoreil.com). Bring your own poles and bait. (The preserve does not allow minnows for bait in order to keep the fish healthy and free of invasive species.)

Each summer, Four Lakes hosts an annual free fishing derby for kids ages 3 to 16 called Hooked on Fun. Kids are able to use loaner equipment to fish during the event. Prizes are awarded for several age groups for the largest fish caught during the event.

Catch, keep, and eat a wide variety of fish!

SPENCER CONSERVATION AREA

899 Appleton Rd, Belvidere
bccdil.org/explore/spencer-conservation-area

Another popular place for fishing is the Spencer Conservation Area. This 350-acre site is bordered by the Kishwaukee River and has two ponds stocked with fish and a mile of river frontage for fishing. There are size and creel limits posted on signage near the fishing areas. You can catch sunfish, bass, and bluegill here. In June each year, the Boone County Conservation District hosts a free kids' fishing derby for ages 5–15 that includes prizes and lunch.

How to be a best mom:

- **Be sure to take a photo with the best catch of the day.**
- **Stop in the Nature Center to see a variety of educational displays.**

LAKE VICTORIA

400 Winnebago Ave., South Beloit

Lake Victoria in South Beloit is a beautiful place to go fishing in a quiet environment. Lake Victoria is a man-made lake stocked with fish, located in City Park. There are catfish, bluegill, black crappie, and bass in the lake. There is a daily rate to fish at Lake Victoria. There is also a walking path and bridge along the lake and a playground for kids to enjoy near the entrance.

How to be a best mom:

- **Pack a lunch and enjoy an outdoor meal at their picnic tables.**
- **Keep having fun outdoors by paying a visit to Nature at the Confluence and stomping in Kelly Creek.**

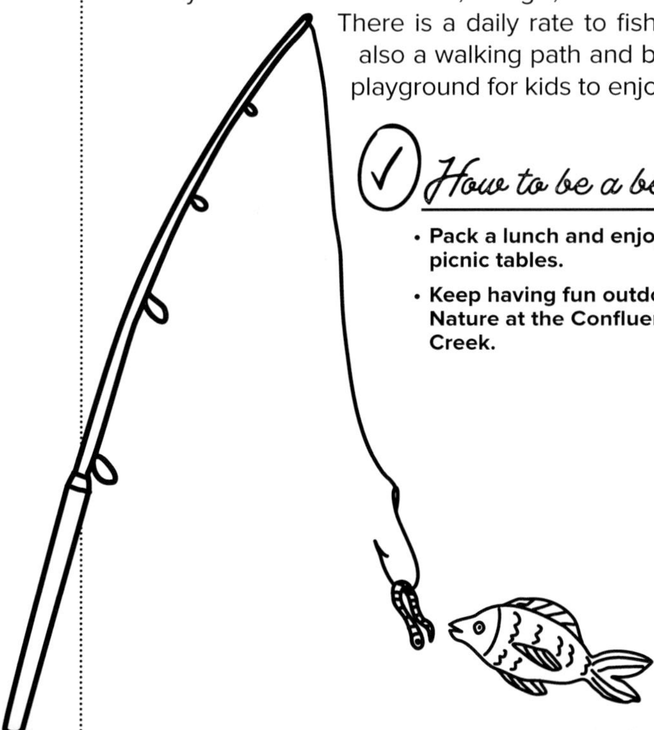

Best Place to Learn to Play Golf

SUNDAY FUNDAY GOLF

Sinnissippi Golf Course | 2003 Arlington Ave. | 815-987-8838
Ingersoll Golf Course | 101 Daisyfield Rd. | 815-987-8834
golfrockford.org

Learn how to putt at Sunday Funday Golf! Every Sunday during golf season, the Rockford Park District offers family-friendly Sunday Funday golf events at two area golf courses. Sinnissippi Golf Course hosts a Sunday Funday at their nine-hole course nestled in the rolling hills of Sinnissippi Park. Ingersoll Golf Course has a driving range option at their wooded, 18-hole course.

Sunday Funday at Sinnissippi Golf Course kicks off Sundays at 3 p.m. Beginners of all ages can enjoy a round of golf for a low cost (around $5 per person). Kids under 14 golf for free. Golf carts are available for a fee, but the course is walkable if families prefer. Sinnissippi is an easier course with a relaxed atmosphere that makes it perfect for beginners. A limited number of clubs are available to borrow. Reservations can be made online through golfrockford.org.

At Ingersoll Golf Course, kids ages 14 and under can hit a bucket of balls every Sunday after 3 p.m. for free. A limited number of clubs are available to borrow free of charge at this location as well. The Rockford Park District provides golf lessons for both kids and families throughout the golf season. They host special events during the year, including youth tournaments like the Tiger Cub Classic and glow nights during the summer.

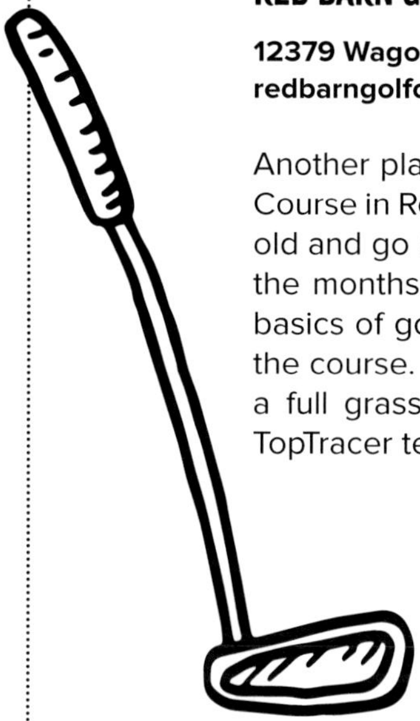

RED BARN GOLF COURSE

12379 Wagon Wheel Rd., Rockton | 815-624-8037
redbarngolfcourse.com

Another place for kids to learn how to golf is Red Barn Golf Course in Rockton. Lessons start for kids as young as 5 years old and go up to age 14. These lessons are only held during the months of June and July each year. Kids will learn the basics of golf, how to putt and drive, and test their skills on the course. Red Barn Golf Course is a nine-hole course with a full grass practice facility. They also have 10 bays with TopTracer technology.

How to be a best mom:

- **See who can drive the farthest on the TopTracer technology.**
- **After a round of golf, stop by Dairyhaus for some homemade ice cream.**

INDOOR SPORTS CENTER

Mercyhealth Sportscore Two | 8800 E Riverside Blvd. | 815-987-8890
mercyhealthsportscore.com/sportscore-two

Throughout the year, the Rockford Park District offers indoor golf lessons at the Indoor Sports Center at Mercyhealth Sportscore Two. These lessons are open to golfers of all ages and abilities. Kids will get focused attention from the professional golf staff and learn how to handle both physical and mental elements of the game. Lessons start at 4 years old and go up to age 14. Adults can also take lessons at the indoor facility.

How to be a best mom:

- **Get the whole family active at the Indoor Sports Center which also has indoor soccer fields.**
- **Grab a bite to eat at the on-site restaurant after your lessons.**

Best Big Party in a Small Town

OLD SETTLERS DAYS

200 Hawick St., Rockton | 815-239-0861
oldsettlersdays.com

Get ready to rock in Rockton! Old Settlers Days, held in Settlers Park, is one big party for all ages in the warm June sun. The event has grown from a street fair in the 1980s to one of the largest music festivals in Northern Illinois. The festival brings in popular country music artists but often has throwback rock stars as well. Premium concerts require tickets, but admission includes the smaller stage that features local bands.

Old Settlers Days takes place from Thursday to Sunday in mid-June each year. The weekend is packed with fun events as well as ways to give back to the community, including an annual blood drive and a charitable 5K run.

Families will have a blast at the festival. On Saturday, a parade kicks off at Hononegah High School before traveling down Main Street, with participants throwing candy the whole way. There are also carnival games, rides, and booths with kids' activities to keep little ones busy. Buy carnival wristbands in advance to give kids unlimited rides within a certain time period. Kiddie rides are available for those ages 2 to 8 as well as faster rides for bigger kids. Parking is free and shuttles are available to take families from Hononegah High School to the fairgrounds. The general admission fee is good for all four days.

BYRONFEST

232 W 2nd St., Byron | 815-234-5500
byronfest.org

Another small town that can throw a big party is Byron! ByronFest happens each summer in early July and includes a ton of fun for the whole family. The three-day festival has live music on two stages from local and national artists. They also have a full carnival midway with rides and games, all the fair food you'd expect, a 5K, a bags tournament, a car show, and a parade. Spending a weekend having fun in Byron should be on your summer fun list.

How to be a best mom:

- **Make a day of it and stop by PrairieFire Golf and Grill for lunch and golf games.**
- **Head to ByronFest on Sunday for free admission on family day.**

WINNEBAGO COUNTY FAIR

500 W 1st St., Pecatonica | 815-239-1641
winnebagocountyfair.com

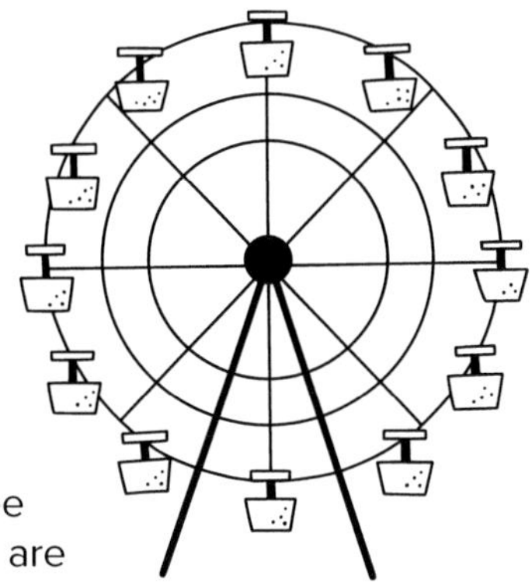

Summer wraps up with the Winnebago County Fair, the last of the area fairs happening the third week of August each year. The Winnebago County Fair brings together fun on the farm with a carnival atmosphere for five days. There are 4-H shows, tractor displays, magic shows, a beauty pageant, and daily entertainment including music from local and touring bands. They also have a midway with games and rides. Much of the entertainment is free during the event, and special deals and discounts are available most days.

How to be a best mom:

- **Save some cash and pick up a MegaPass for your kids to ride at select locations a few weeks before the fair kicks off.**
- **End your summer with a funnel cake or elephant ear!**

Best Way to Have Fun Learning about Agriculture

BOONE COUNTY FAIR

8847 IL-76, Belvidere | 815-544-2900
boonecountyfair.com

Learn about livestock while having a blast at the Boone County Fair! The Boone County Fair is one of the biggest, and longest-running, county fairs in the area. Though the fair has changed since it began in 1855, the main draw is still its agriculture and livestock exhibits, with over 3,000 animals, from rabbits to draft horses, and 6,000 agriculture exhibits showcasing corn, cakes, quilts, and more.

More than 45 buildings, which house everything from petting zoos to food vendors, offer new surprises for visitors. There's also a traditional midway stacked with games where kids can win prizes. Rides include a carousel of cars for the littlest adventurer and bigger thrills like the Zipper for adults and teens. In the Entertainment Pavilion, singers and local bands play to the crowds.

Kids can learn how to milk a cow and see chicks being hatched, sheep being sheared, and horses being saddled or hitched to a wagon. The farmers and exhibitors are happy to explain what they're doing and often let kids lend a hand. A county fair wouldn't be complete without delectable food! Don't miss the cream puffs and fireman doughnuts—both are crowd favorites. Be sure to arrive hungry to try pulled pork sandwiches, baked potatoes with all the toppings, corn on the cob, and more.

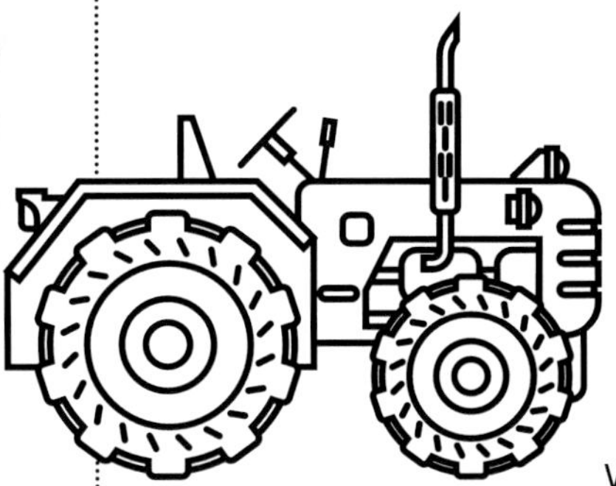

ANNUAL FARM BREAKFAST

1925 S Meridian Rd. | 815-962-0653
winnebagoboonefarmbureau.org

Each June, the Winnebago-Boone Farm Bureau invites families to join them for an Annual Farm Breakfast. Every year, the farm breakfast is hosted at a different farm in Winnebago or Boone County. The farm breakfast event includes kids' activities, tractor rides, wagon rides, milking demonstrations, live music, and, of course, breakfast! The breakfast is an all-you-can-eat affair with pancakes, whole hog sausage, applesauce, ice cream, and more. Families can enjoy a fun morning learning more about how a working farm runs!

✓ *How to be a best mom:*

- **If you have a high school student interested in a career in agriculture, have them apply for a scholarship through the Winnebago-Boone Farm Bureau Foundation.**
- **Arrive early to insure you get to try all of the delicious food.**

4-H IN WINNEBAGO COUNTY

1925 S Meridian Rd.
facebook.com/profile.php?id=100070332420872

4-H in Winnebago County offers kids a chance to learn about science, healthy living, civic engagement, and agriculture. Kids complete hands-on projects, in their areas of interest, that can be entered into the Winnebago County Fair. Kids can also raise and show livestock including horses, cows, poultry, rabbits, dogs, and cats. The local 4-H chapter offers a variety of programs throughout the year as well as regular club meetings. Kids ages 5–18 are welcome to join.

✓ *How to be a best mom:*

- **Save the date for the 4-H Fun Day held in March each year. Kids get a chance to learn about 4-H at this event.**
- **Sign up little ones for Wee Naturalists group which includes a storytime, activity, and hike.**

Best Place to Wrap Up the Summer

WINNEBAGO COUNTY FAIR

500 W 1st St., Pecatonica | 815-239-1641
winnebagocountyfair.com

Say goodbye to summer at the Winnebago County Fair! This fair wraps up each summer in the Rockford area with a big blowout at the end of August. The event has been held at the Winnebago County Fairgrounds since 1921. The fairgrounds feature over 85,000 square feet of indoor exhibit space and a 4,000-seat grandstand.

The Winnebago County Fair has something for everyone in the family to enjoy. The fair starts with a 4-H exhibit where members show the animals they have raised throughout the year. An annual beauty pageant crowns the Winnebago County Fair Queen. No fair is complete without a midway filled with games and rides. Thrill seekers will love the roller coasters like the Fireball and topsy-turvy rides like the Zipper. Buy a Megapass for unlimited rides during selected time periods.

Rodeos, demolition derby, magic shows, and live music are scheduled all day long. On Kids Day, which happens once per fair season, the schedule is packed with child-friendly entertainment like puppet shows, magicians, and acrobats that will surprise and delight kids and their parents. Don't miss fair food classics like funnel cakes decked out in powdered sugar and syrup toppings of your choice as well as cotton candy, corn on the cob, street tacos, and more. Wash it down with a lemon shake-up.

LABOR DAY PARADE

City of Rockford | 425 E State St., Rockford | 815-977-7050
rockfordbuzz.com/labor-day-parade

Labor Day is often thought of as the official end of summer, and Rockford knows how to send it out with a bang. The Labor Day parade is held each year by the Rockford United Labor AFL-CIO. The parade starts at the intersection of 6th and 7th Streets in downtown Rockford and then continues to the Davis Park entrance. Bring a chair and find a spot along the downtown route. Kids will love seeing the dozens of patriotically decorated Jeeps from Screw City Jeeps as well as fire trucks and other community vehicles. Bring a bag because many of the participants throw candy to the kids!

✓ *How to be a best mom:*

- **Arrive at least one hour before the parade kicks off to get the best seats in downtown Rockford.**
- **Head to Davis Park after the parade for live music and a car show.**

UP IN THE AIR FESTIVAL

1111 Fairgrounds Rd., Belvidere | 815-547-9557
belviderepark.org/parks-facilities/prairie-fields-sports-park

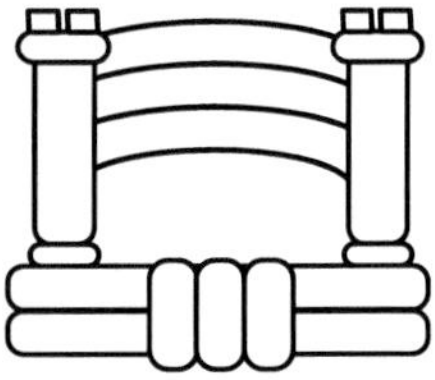

Wave goodbye to summer as it floats past like a kite in the wind at Belvidere's Up in the Air festival. This annual festival is held in early September at Prairie Field Sports Park and runs for four hours. The event includes dozens of colorful kites flying through the air, which is a spectacular site to see. In addition to the kite-flying demos, there are inflatables, face painting, games, crafts, and food trucks on-site. It's a beautiful way to end the summer.

✓ *How to be a best mom:*

- **Buy an unlimited activity wristband for access to most of the paid events at the festival.**
- **Bring your own kite and get tips on how to best fly it or pick one up at the park.**

Best Place to Embrace Your Heritage

FESTA ITALIANA

4000 St. Francis Dr. | 815-289-7704
festaitalianarockford.com

Everyone's a little bit Italian every August, *capiche*? Each summer, Festa Italiana (Italian Fest) is held at Boylan Catholic High School. Festa is a three-day event celebrating all things Italian. It benefits the Greater Rockford Italian American Association, a nonprofit that promotes Italian culture.

The festival offers a variety of traditional and updated Italian dishes made fresh. Families can indulge in classics like Italian beef and peppers, arancini, meatballs, and a variety of pasta and sauces. Crowd favorites are the savory fried ravioli, sweet and refreshing granita in multiple flavors, and Italian cookies. Beer, wine, and drinks like lemon shake-ups are available. Musicians and Italian dancing troupes perform onstage.

The festival includes a midway with carnival games and rides for kids. There are several kiddie rides for those 7 and under, a fun house, and rides for bigger kids like a swinging boat. The Kids Craft area allows kids to design pasta necklaces and other crafts to take home. Adults can enter a boccie ball tournament that runs on Friday and Saturday and awards the top three teams for men and women with a cash prize. All activities and food are purchased with tickets, available at the festival. A family pass deal can be purchased on Festa Italiana's website before the festival that includes unlimited ride wristbands and food tickets.

MIDSOMMAR FEST

404 S 3rd St. | 815-963-5559
swedishhistorical.org/midsommar.html

Get into the Swedish spirit at Midsommar Fest held annually at Erlander Home Museum. Each June, Swedes gather for a full day of festivities celebrating the midpoint of harvest season and summer solstice. This beautiful festival includes a traditional raising of the maypole, performances from Nordic folk dancers, live music, games and crafts for kids, shopping, an architectural walking tour, and a Swedish pancake eating contest. You'll be saying *usch då* if you miss this one!

✓ *How to be a best mom:*

- **Enjoy more Swedish food at Stockholm Inn or Swedish Pancake House where you can get authentic Swedish pancakes.**
- **Save the date for The Norwegian's SnoMarket which happens each December and turns the back alley of the restaurant into a Nordic fishing village and open air market.**

POLISH FEST

201 Buckbee St. | 815-965-3913
artsforeveryone.com/event/polish-fest

O jejku! Get ready for some delicious food and entertaining performances at Polish Fest! Polish Fest takes place in August each year at St. Stanislaus Kostka Church. This event has been held for over 40 years to celebrate Polish culture. The event includes a Polish and English mass, live music from local bands and Midwest acts, games for kids, and folk dance. Of course, you can also sample Polish food including several varieties of pierogi, potato pancakes, polish sausage, sauerkraut, Polish beef, and light and fluffy pastries.

✓ *How to be a best mom:*

- **If you're looking for authentic Polish food, head to the Polish Deli on Charles Street for variety of dishes.**
- **Learn more about the first Polish immigrants in Rockford at the Ethnic Heritage Museum.**

Best Way to Celebrate America's Birthday

ROCKFORD'S FOURTH OF JULY CELEBRATION

728 N Prospect St., Ste. 107
facebook.com/rockford4thofjulycelebration

It's red, white, and boom in downtown Rockford on the Fourth! Rockford's Fourth of July celebration is the area's largest parade and fireworks show. It was started in 1963 by World War II veteran Joe Marino. His legacy lives on through the committee and the *Mr. Fourth of July* statue and plaque on the corner of State and Water Streets.

The Fourth of July celebration starts off with a joyous parade through the streets of downtown Rockford. The parade includes motorcycles, patriotically decorated Jeeps from Screw City Jeeps, emergency vehicles, and floats. Most of the floats throw candy into the crowd, so be sure to bring along bags. The parade includes performances from high school drum corps, dance companies, and theater troupes. The fun continues with live entertainment on four stages in Davis Park.

Each year, the fireworks show gets bigger and better. In recent years, they've used a pyrotechnic team who worked on the Super Bowl. Though the fireworks are visible from locations throughout the city, the real fun happens in Davis Park. A free children's area has balloon twisters, stilt walkers, glitter tattoos, and yard games. Food trucks and drink vendors selling both nonalcoholic and alcoholic beverages are on-site. The fireworks begin at 9:30 p.m. and go for 30 minutes of nonstop excitement.

KIRKLAND'S FOURTH OF JULY

kirklandfourthofjuly.com

The largest fireworks display in the area takes place in Kirkland, a short drive from Rockford. For more than 75 years, Kirkland has been lighting up the night sky on the Fourth with an impressive firework show for all ages. The fireworks show is just one part of the three-day Fourth of July celebration that the small town puts on. The festivities include live music, a tractor show, a bags tournament, and a parade. Bring chairs, blankets, and bug spray to enjoy the fireworks, which are set off at dusk!

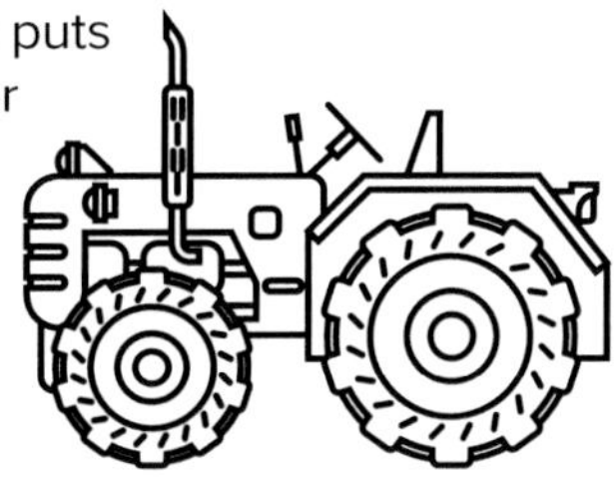

✓ *How to be a best mom:*

- **Pack a lunch and plan to spend the entire day enjoying the fun in Kirkland on the Fourth.**
- **Buy a carnival wristband for unlimited rides on select days and times during the weekend.**

POP ON THE ROCKS

1160 Riverside Dr., Beloit, WI | 608-364-2890

For a fireworks show that rivals any other, head over the state line to Riverside Park in Beloit for their Pop on the Rocks event. Prior to the fireworks display, the Beloit Janesville Symphony Orchestra plays a free Independence Day concert with patriotic songs as well as a medley that recognizes each branch of the military. The fireworks display itself is over 30 minutes of continuous dazzling fireworks. The surrounding neighborhoods shoot off their own fireworks, which leads to bursts of color in every direction. It's a sight to see!

✓ *How to be a best mom:*

- **Park in the Beloit Public Library parking lot for a less crowded view of the fireworks.**
- **When it's not the 4th, you can still catch fireworks after many of the Beloit Sky Carp games.**

Best Place to Catch a Baseball Game

RIVETS STADIUM

4503 Interstate Blvd., Loves Park
815-240-4159
northwoodsleague.com/rockford-rivets

Summer and baseball go together like peanut butter and jelly! Rockford is lucky to have its very own team, the Rockford Rivets, continuing the legacy of baseball in Rockford. The Rivets play their home games at Rivets Stadium. The Rivets are part of the Northwoods League playing teams based in Indiana, Michigan, and Wisconsin.

Families can catch a baseball game during the Rivets' season, which spans from late May to mid-August. The games are lively and fun, and there isn't a bad seat in the house. Promotions are often geared toward families, including Kids Day, which offers an afternoon game on a weekday. Bobbleheads and blankets are given away at select games. Several times during the summer, fireworks shoot off after the game, especially around the Fourth of July.

The Rockford Rivets offer youth baseball camp during the summer, which is geared toward kids ages 6 to 12. These camps are led by the college-aged players and team coaches. Really want to get involved with the Rivets? Become a host family and have one of the Rivets players live with you for the summer. Host families provide food and shelter for the player and in return get season tickets. Rockford's rich history with baseball is reason enough to head out and support the Rivets!

Rivets games are lively and fun!

ABC SUPPLY STADIUM

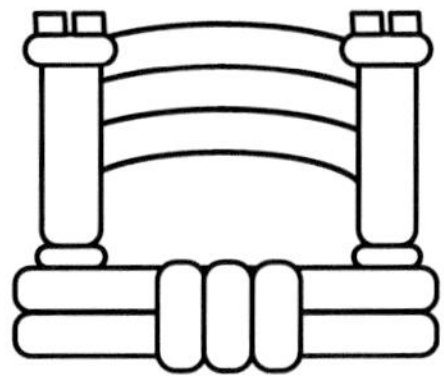

217 Shirland Ave., Beloit, WI | 608-362-2272
https://www.milb.com/beloit

Head north to Beloit to catch a fantastically fun Beloit Sky Carp game! The Beloit Sky Carp are a Minor League baseball team in the Midwest League. They play home games in the beautiful ABC Supply Stadium. Sky Carp games are high-energy with special deals and promotions happening throughout the season including their Copa de la Diversion series where the Sky Carp play as the Paletas. Kids will have a blast enjoying the bounce house, games, and foot race on the field after the third inning.

✓ *How to be a best mom:*

- **On Sundays, bring your own mitt and ball to play catch on the field after the game.**
- **While you're there, be sure to stop by the Kids Zone to jump in the bounce house for free.**

IMPACT FIELD

9850 Balmoral Ave., Rosemont | 847-636-5450
thechicagodogs.com/explore-impact

Take a short drive to Rosemont to see the Chicago Dogs play at Impact Field. The Chicago Dogs are part of the American Association of Independent Professional Baseball. Their games are entertaining for the whole family. Throughout the week, they have special events like theme night Saturdays with fireworks, giveaways, and Wiener Wednesdays with $1 hot dogs and the team playing as the Chicago Wieners. It's worth the drive to catch a game this summer!

✓ *How to be a best mom:*

- **Attend a Saturday game to enjoy theme night and see the fireworks.**
- **Head to Impact Field during the holiday season for an incredible outdoor Christmas light display.**

Best Place to Welcome Fall

EDWARDS APPLE ORCHARD

7061 Centerville Rd., Poplar Grove | 815-765-2234
edwardsorchard.farm

It's not really fall until you've had your first bite of a warm apple cider doughnut from Edwards! Edwards Apple Orchard in Poplar Grove is a fall tradition for Rockford families that has been lovingly maintained and run by the same family for over 60 years.

Families can start off their visit with a wagon ride into the orchard to pick their own apples. Varieties include Honeycrisp, Gala, Jonamac, and Autumn Beauty. In September, UPick fields open for berries and pumpkins. Edwards is known for many things, but their apple cider doughnuts are a favorite. These soft and delicious pastries are fried and then coated in cinnamon and sugar and served up warm. Edwards's homemade apple cider completes the perfect pair. The cider is sold in half pints, pints, and gallons to take home. The Cider Cellar also serves up pork sandwiches, homemade apple pie, and other drinks.

Edwards has a petting zoo with goats, lambs, and other barnyard animals that kids can feed. Kids can play on a pirate ship, get lost in a maze, take a pony ride, and pretend to be part of the tiny play village in the kids' area. Live music is popular on weekends. Don't miss walking through the museum and learning more about this family farm.

ROSCOE'S FALL FESTIVAL

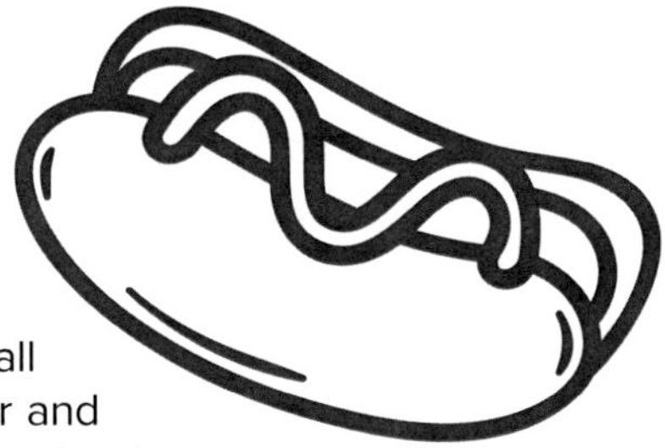

roscoelionsclubil.com

If you're not quite ready to say goodbye to summer yet, Roscoe Lions Club's annual Fall Festival is the perfect branch between summer and fall. The festival is held at the beginning of September but still has a summer fair feel. The three-day event includes a midway with games and rides, live music from local bands, fair food including funnel cakes and hot dogs, raffles, local vendors, and a bingo tent where games are played all day long. There is also a parade on the last day of the festival that officially welcomes in fall.

How to be a best mom:

- **Park in the surrounding neighborhoods or near the YMCA then walk down to Main Street to get the best spot for the parade.**
- **Dress your kids up and bring them to the Kiddie Costume parade on Saturday for a chance to win prizes.**

AUTUMN AT THE ARBORETUM

2715 S Main St. | 815-965-8146
klehm.org

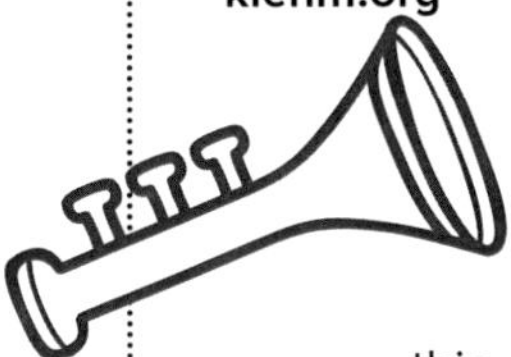

A beautiful place to see the splendor of fall is Klehm Arboretum. Their annual Autumn at the Arboretum event celebrates the season with two days of fun. Klehm waives the admission fee for this event so everyone gets in free all weekend long. Visitors are encouraged to explore the 155 acres for signs of fall as well as enjoy the live music, activities, and entertainment. There are free educational lectures and classes throughout the weekend. Sunday is always Family Fun Day with kids' activities including a hay bale maze and community booths.

How to be a best mom:

- **Be sure to bring your phone so your kids can participate in the digital scavenger hunt.**
- **Kids can bring their carved pumpkins to enter the kids' pumpkin carving contest.**

Best Place to Go Apple Picking

CURRAN'S ORCHARD

6385 Kilburn Ave. | 815-963-7848
curransorchard.com

Pick a peck of apples at Curran's Orchard! Curran's is a quaint and cute apple orchard on Rockford's west side. Curran's offers seasonal favorites like award-winning cider and pies. One of the things that sets Curran's apart is their commitment to using one-third of the typical amount of chemicals when growing their apples. They offer 17 varieties including Jonathan, Jonagold, Rome Beauty, Fuji, Granny Smith, and Honeycrisp. Curran's also offers weekday field trips for schools and homeschoolers.

Kids can sit on a real tractor and meet barnyard animals including pigs and goats at the orchard. Pellets to feed the animals are available for purchase. Younger kids will like the straw-bale corn maze that they can safely explore without getting lost. Bigger kids will enjoy the giant climbing bales that they can scale to get a bird's-eye view of the farm. Kids can test their aim while firing apples with the apple launcher.

Plenty of picnic tables are located around the grounds where families can relax and enjoy a snack. Photo-op spots to take yearly portraits include the adorable scarecrow where kids can measure how much they've grown since last year. Shop the store and bakery for doughnuts, apples, syrups, jams, pies, salsas, and salad dressings as well as cute gifts, home decor, and some small toys.

EDWARDS APPLE ORCHARD WEST

8218 Cemetery Rd., Winnebago | 815-963-2261
edwardsorchardwest.com

Make it an orchard hop and head to Edwards Apple Orchard West for more fun! Edwards West is often a less crowded option when it comes to Rockford area orchards. It's a great place to visit with kids because they have slides, tractors to sit on, and lots of green space to run around. There is also a petting zoo with animals to feed including goats, turkeys, and more. On weekends and holidays, families can take a wagon ride through the orchard and go apple picking!

How to be a best mom:

- **Be sure to have quarters on hand to buy animal feed for the petting barn.**
- **Bring cash for the wagon ride around the orchard.**

VALLEY ORCHARD

811 E State St., Cherry Valley | 815-332-9696
thevalleyorchard.com

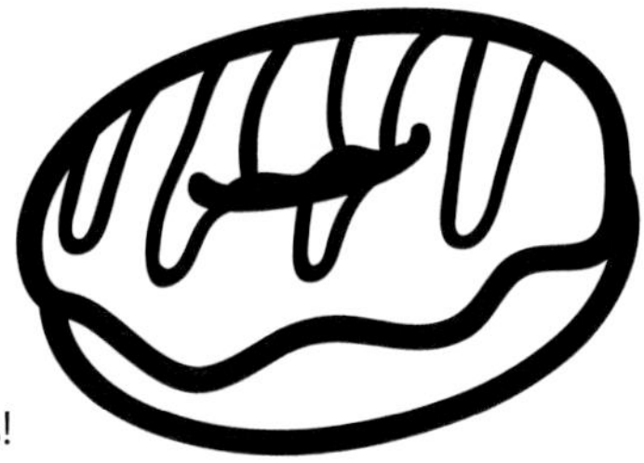

Located in Cherry Valley, Valley Orchard is a 35-acre orchard with 5,000 apple trees. Valley Orchard not only has traditional cinnamon and sugar apple cider doughnuts, but they also offer a glazed apple cider doughnut that is delicious! Throughout the late summer and early fall, you can pick a variety of berries, apples, and pumpkins at the orchard. They also have a small play area perfect for toddlers and preschoolers and plenty of picnic tables to relax and enjoy the beautiful scenery.

How to be a best mom:

- **Enjoy your donuts outside at one of the seating areas overlooking the orchard.**
- **Take a yearly photo of your kid with the adorable apple measuring stick.**

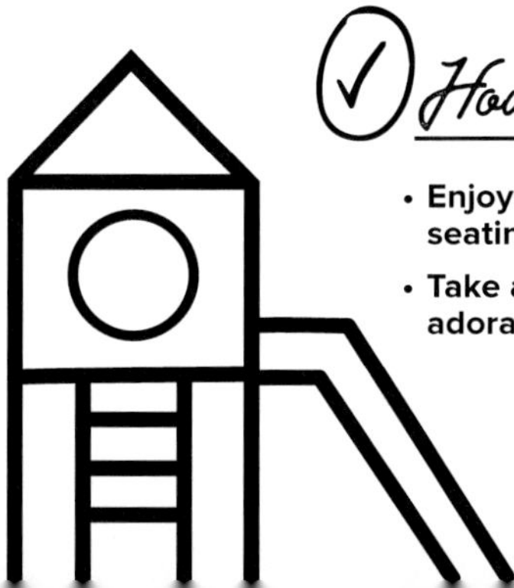

Best Place to Find Local Art

ROCKFORD ART MUSEUM

711 N Main St. | 815-968-2787
greenwichvillageartfair.com

Shop local and find amazing artwork! The Greenwich Village Art Fair has been held each September at Rockford Art Museum since 1948. It is the longest-running art fair of its kind in the Midwest. All artwork on display must be original and produced entirely by the exhibiting artist. No reproductions or mass-produced work are allowed.

The Greenwich Village Art Fair is a two-day experience located outdoors at the Riverfront Museum Park. The fair accepts no more than 155 juried artists who compete for cash awards. The artists featured compete in the following categories: ceramics, drawing/works on paper, fiber, furniture, leather, glass, jewelry, mixed media, painting, paper, photography, printmaking, sculpture, and wood. Artists are also able to sell their works at the fair. Families can expect to see hundreds of pieces of quality artwork made by local artisans.

The fair has live music and food and drinks for sale. The fair also has children's tents with free activities, which vary each year. In the past, kids have been able to paint watercolors on a canvas, create artwork from paper, and try their hand at printmaking. The Greenwich Village Art Fair is a kaleidoscope of colors that showcases Rockford and the surrounding area's many talented artists and makers. Held entirely in a paved parking lot, the fair is accessible for both wheelchairs and strollers.

ROCKFORD'S ARTSCENE

713 E State St. | 815-963-6765
artsforeveryone.com/artscene

Another place to find local art to brighten up your home is Rockford's ArtScene. This biannual tradition, held by the Rockford Area Arts Council, has been going on since 1987. Each spring and fall, area businesses open up their walls to host local artists of all kinds for a two-night gallery walk. Artists offer their work for purchase including paintings, sculptures, prints, photography, jewelry, fiber arts, and more. The Fall ArtScene happens in October each year and the Spring ArtScene happens in April. The ArtScene is a great way to introduce your kids to an appreciation for local arts.

✓ *How to be a best mom:*

- **Pick up a booklet with map at the Rockford Area Arts Council before heading to the locations.**
- **Enjoy a dinner at kid-friendly Woodfire Pizza after checking out the art downtown.**

JR FINALLY ART STUDIO AND GALLERY

210 W Main St., Rockton | 815-742-4631
jillraefinallyart.com/index.html

Head to charming downtown Rockton to shop at JR Finally Art Studio and Gallery. The shop offers a variety of both prints and original artwork by owner Jill Rae Martin-Golden. Her beautiful florals, cityscapes, and colorful pet portraits would make a lovely addition to anyone's home. Jill also offers custom art made from a high-resolution photo. These works of art would be a wonderful gift for Mother's Day, Father's Day, or a grandparent's birthday. Jill also offers painting classes for kids for your budding Picasso.

✓ *How to be a best mom:*

- **Stop by the get a make and take project during Christmas Walk, Pelican Fest, and other Rockton celebrations.**
- **Sign up your 7–12 year old for weekly art classes held at the studio all year long.**

Best Place to Glow in the Dark

GLOW IN THE GARDENS

1354 N 2nd St. | 815-987-8858
nicholasconservatory.com/events/glow-in-the-garden-festival

Have a glowing good time at Glow in the Garden! Glow in the Garden is an annual festival held in September at Nicholas Conservatory & Gardens. The gardens are decorated in colorful lights and the vibe is festive.

One of coolest parts of the event is the glowing lantern release. Families can purchase lanterns in advance or buy them at the event. A station with markers is available where the lanterns can be decorated before being set loose in the Eclipse Lagoon. Families are encouraged to wear black-light reactive clothing and glow-stick jewelry to light up the night. Glowing items are available for purchase, including light wands, headbands, glasses, necklaces, and more.

Around 7 p.m., the 5K race (3.1 miles) on the Rock River Recreation Path kicks off. Attendees can cheer on the racers. A Kids Fun Run of approximately 200 meters starts at the entrance sign. In the pavilion, families can use black-light reactive chalk to write messages on the ground. Admission to the event is free, but some activities have a small charge. Families can enjoy food from local food trucks, and adults can purchase mixed drinks from VeeDubs Mobile Bar. Free trolley rides on a decked-out, lit-up Trolley 36 leave every few minutes to travel along the Rock River Recreation Path.

COSMIC BOWLING

7171 Cherryvale N Blvd.
thecherrybowlonline.com

For a glowing good time any time of the year, head to the Cherry Bowl. Every Friday and Saturday night, the Cherry Bowl offers Cosmic Bowl where they turn off the overhead lights, turn on the black lights, and make everything glow! There are also spotlights, strobe lights, and fog that complement the upbeat pop music to make for a super fun night of bowling. Cosmic bowling is fun for all ages! They also offer a Cosmic Bowling birthday party option.

How to be a best mom:

- **Book your kid's next birthday party at Cherry Bowl and include a cosmic bowling portion.**
- **Wear your best day-glo outfits and accessories when you go bowling.**

THE POTTERY LOUNGE

6059 E State St. | 815-977-3937
thepotterylounge.com

Create some glow-in-the-dark art at the Pottery Lounge. The Pottery Lounge hosts tons of fun events, but this one might be the most eye-catching. Neon Glow Night allows families to choose either a pre-drawn or blank canvas to paint on beneath the black light. They provide the black-light-reactive paint and you provide the creativity! Wearing glowing clothes is encouraged. Tickets are required for all of the Pottery Lounge's special events and you can find them on their website.

How to be a best mom:

- **Check The Pottery Lounge's website for fun, family-friendly events all year long.**
- **Spend a day off school painting and making memories with your kids.**

Best Way to Welcome the Spooky Season

LINDBERG PUMPKIN PATCH

3178 IL 173, Caledonia | 815-990-7034
lindbergpumpkinpatch.com

Have a scary good time at the pumpkin patch! Lindberg Pumpkin Patch offers pick-your-own pumpkins and Halloween fun. The U-pick patch has more than 50 varieties of pumpkins in shades ranging from white to dark orange and even an unusual blue pumpkin. The pumpkin patch is open daily from mid-September through Halloween.

Spend the day having fun with an all-inclusive wristband purchase. Kids can visit and feed animals in the petting zoo, take a wagon ride, be pulled in the pumpkin train, climb on a spider web made of ropes, and get immersed in thousands of corn kernels in the corn bin. Brave souls can try to make their way through the haunted shed. One of the biggest attractions is the seven-acre corn maze. On the weekends, the pumpkin patch brings out a corn cannon so kids can launch corn sky-high.

Pumpkin-themed treats are available at the Pumpkin Café including freshly made pumpkin doughnuts, pumpkin bars, and pumpkin breads. The Goblin Grill offers up burgers, brats, and cheese curds. The Corn Shack specializes in roasted sweet corn and popcorn. The Spud Hut serves up baked potatoes with topping options. Throughout the season, the Lindberg Pumpkin Patch hosts events including the Witches Ball, a costumed dance for kids and parents in October.

TINKER'S TRUNK OR TREAT

411 Kent St. | 815-964-2424
tinkercottage.com

Nothing says spooky season like a Trunk or Treat. Tinker Swiss Cottage and Museum is the perfect place to host one because of its spooky history–it's rumored to be haunted by the ghosts of the Tinker family! Every October, Tinker Swiss Cottage puts on a fun, family-friendly Trunk or Treat outdoors that includes at least a dozen decorated trunks from local businesses. They also have live music, crafts, and free guided tours of the first floor of Tinker Swiss Cottage. Be sure to come in costume! For an extra-scary experience, teens and parents may enjoy the haunted tours offered throughout October!

How to be a best mom:

- **Don't miss walking around the back of the Tinker Swiss Cottage and to see the lovely view of Kent Creek.**
- **Get into the spirit by wearing coordinating family costumes to the Trunk or Treat!**

ALL HALLOW'S EVE

6799 Guilford Rd. | 815-397-9112
midwayvillage.com

Celebrate Halloween at Midway Village Museum's annual All Hallow's Eve celebration. This full-day event takes place outdoors in the Victorian Village. Families are encouraged to dress up in their Halloween costumes and trick-or-treat from local businesses stationed in the historic buildings throughout the village. Inside the barn, kids can warm up and do crafts to take home. Other attractions include a not-so-scary haunted house, live music, and food trucks on-site. The event is a Halloween classic and should not be missed!

How to be a best mom:

- **Be sure to bring a large bag or bucket because there are lots of treats to collect.**
- **Stop in the barn for Halloween themed crafts that you can make on the spot.**

Best Sporting Event on Ice

ROCKFORD ICEHOGS GAME

300 Elm St. | 815-968-5222
thebmocenter.com

The fans bring the energy and the Hogs play to win! The Rockford IceHogs have been Rockford's professional ice hockey team since 1999. Their season runs from October through April and typically consists of 72 games, though there may be more if the team makes it into a cup playoff. The games are held in the BMO Center in downtown Rockford.

Games are well-attended, fast-paced, and entertaining. Throughout the season, the IceHogs offer promotions at their games, giving away things like T-shirts, bobbleheads, and blankets to the first 1,000 fans in the door. The BMO Center also sells a variety of IceHogs merchandise, including hats, foam fingers, hoodies, jerseys, and pucks. During the games, kids can keep an eye out for the IceHogs' mascot, Hammy, who often walks around the stands and takes pictures with fans.

When the IceHogs score a goal, the stadium erupts into cheers and a loud siren wails while the lights flash. Though the games are a lot of fun, they can be overwhelming for a child with sensory issues. Consider bringing noise-canceling headphones or earplugs if a family member is sensitive to loud noises. The concession stands are open throughout the game selling fan favorites like hot dogs, nachos, slushies, soda, alcoholic beverages, and more.

SPRING ICE SHOW

4150 N Perryville Rd., Loves Park | 815-969-4069
icerockford.com/carlson

Each spring, the talented athletes of figure skating show off their skills at the Spring Ice Show at Carlson Ice Arena. This annual show is a chance for more than 100 local skaters of all ages from Rockford Park District's programs to perform on ice. The show includes group, solo, specialty, and synchronized music performances. Each year, the show has a theme. In addition, each year, the show has special guests such as nationally ranked skaters who also perform. Tickets are available for the public to see this amazing show.

How to be a best mom:

- **Sign your kids up to learn how to ice skate through the Rockford Park District. Lessons start at 18 months old.**
- **Get some hot chocolate and a snack at the concession stand while you watch the show.**

CHICAGO WOLVES GAME

6920 N Mannheim Rd., Rosemont | 847-635-6601
rosemont.com/allstate

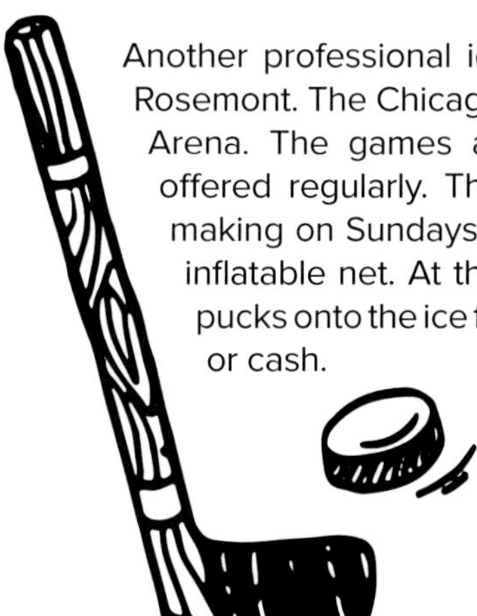

Another professional ice hockey team is only a short drive away in Rosemont. The Chicago Wolves play their home games at the Allstate Arena. The games are fun and entertaining with themed nights offered regularly. There are also kid activities including free sign making on Sundays and a game where kids can hit a puck into an inflatable net. At the end of the games, families can toss squishy pucks onto the ice for a chance to win Chicago Wolves merchandise or cash.

How to be a best mom:

- **Visit the Kids Zone to take photos with the replica locker room and jerseys.**
- **Check out the extensive collection of Chicago Wolves merchandise for sale.**

Best Place to Celebrate the Most Wonderful Time of the Year

STROLL ON STATE

102 N Main St. | 800-521-0849
gorockford.com/stroll-on-state

Welcome the holiday season at Stroll on State! Many families' favorite event of the year, Stroll on State started in 2012 as a way for the community to gather in downtown Rockford for a Christmas tree lighting, live music, and shopping. It has since become the official kickoff of the holiday season as well as a huge tourist event for the Rockford area.

Stroll on State is a whole-day experience that begins with a parade through downtown. Expect to see fire trucks, police vehicles, dozens of decorated Jeeps, and numerous large-scale balloons. The parade wraps up with an appearance from Santa. After the parade, the festivities begin, many of which are free to do. Families can take a horse-drawn carriage ride around town, play games provided by the Rockford Park District, and watch a holiday movie. Two markets have more than 50 vendors selling holiday items and gifts.

Don't miss the hot chocolate and s'mores stations where families can buy a cup of cocoa to warm up with and a sticky treat. Several stages have live performances from local bands, theater groups, and dance companies. There is also an ice carver who saws ice blocks into detailed sculptures. In years past, these events have had lots of fun activities for kids, including writing Santa a letter at City Hall and getting a photo with him as he walks around the event.

WILLIAMS TREE FARM

4661 Yale Bridge Rd., Rockton | 815-624-7579
williamstreefarm.com

If you want to cut down your own tree and see Santa, Williams Tree Farm is the place to go. Williams Tree Farm has been a staple in the community for over 70 years. There are often special events held at the farm, especially during the weekends, and Santa and Mrs. Claus can be visited for free throughout the holiday season. Families can cut down their own trees or buy a pre-cut one. Don't forget to stop and see the reindeer, camel, and other animals at the Children's Farm!

✓ *How to be a best mom:*

- **Check Williams Tree Farm's website for information on free holiday storytimes and caroling.**
- **Be prepared to wait to see Santa! Visit earlier in the season for shorter wait times.**

CHRISTMAS TOWN

3088 Flora Rd., Belvidere | 815-547-4852
summerfieldfarmandzoo.secureserversites.net

Get up close and personal with Santa's flight crew at Summerfield Zoo. During November and December, the zoo is transformed into Christmas Town, an immersive holiday experience. Kids can get a close look at live reindeer, see Santa and tell him what they want for Christmas, and enjoy some hot cocoa while viewing the animals on the farm. There are also Flight School demonstrations and the chance to get a photo with a baby reindeer. Tickets are required for this magical experience!

✓ *How to be a best mom:*

- **Check out the reindeer in the stables and pick which one is your favorite.**
- **Stop by the pond and count how many types of birds you can spot.**

Best Escape to a Christmas Village

ROCKTON CHRISTMAS WALK

Rockton Village Hall | 110 E Main St., Rockton | 815-624-0935
rocktonchristmaswalk.com

Celebrate the most wonderful time of year in picturesque downtown Rockton! Rockton is located about 20 minutes north of Rockford toward the Wisconsin border. It's a quaint village with an adorable downtown filled with thriving local shops including Dairyhaus, DeeDee's Coffee Shop, Frosted Farmhouse, and Taylor and Max. Every December, Rockton holds its annual Christmas Walk, a wonderful weekend of Christmas-themed fun.

The Rockton Christmas Walk is a Hallmark movie come to life. This delightful celebration held the first weekend of December, is packed with festivities for all ages, including some for adults only. The event kicks off with lighted displays in Settlers Park on Friday night. Also on Friday night, there is typically an event for adults like dueling pianos or an ugly sweater bar crawl. The fun continues with a pancake breakfast with Santa on Saturday morning, craft and bake sales throughout the day, pictures with Santa, horse-drawn carriage rides, a s'more roasting station, and more. Saturday evening's parade is the coolest part of the celebration with dozens of lit-up and decorated floats and cars driving down Main Street.

The weekend wraps up with an annual Hot Cocoa Crawl on Sunday. This event allows families to take a commemorative mug to numerous local shops and try their hot cocoa samples. After families have tasted all of the yummy flavors, they can vote for their favorite.

LIGHT UP THE PARKS HOLIDAY PARADE

Loves Park City Hall | 100 Heart Blvd., Loves Park
Machesney Park Town Center | 8760 N 2nd St., Machesney Park
lightuptheparksparade.com

The parks welcome the holiday season with the Light Up the Parks Holiday Parade. This parade runs through both Loves Park and Machesney Park with tree lightings at Loves Park City Hall and Machesney Park Town Center. There are also fireworks before the parade starts. The parade is filled with lit-up floats from local businesses. At the end of the parade, kids can watch Santa and Mrs. Claus arrive and bring their letters for Santa to drop off in the mailbox.

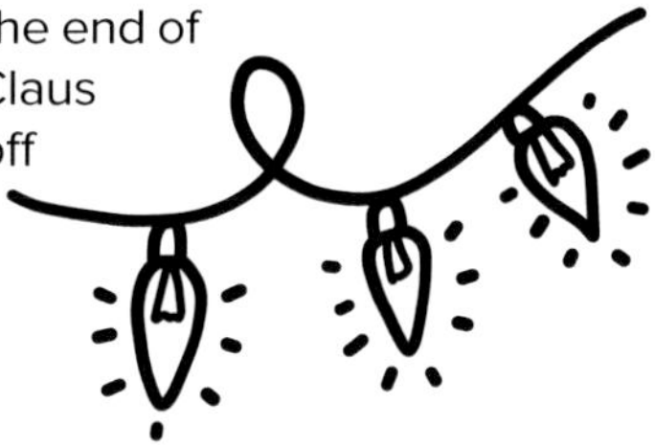

✓ *How to be a best mom:*

- **Head to Elm Avenue to get a good spot for the parade. Bring your own chairs and blankets to stay warm while you wait.**
- **Find a spot near the Christmas tree at Machesney Park Town Center for the best view of Santa and Mrs. Claus.**

HAPPY HOLIDAY RAILWAY

7000 Olson Rd., Union | 815-923-4391
irm.org

Get into the Christmas spirit with a holiday train ride complete with Santa on board! The Happy Holiday Railway at Illinois Railway Museum is a 40-minute train ride through the winter countryside with Santa. There are treats and hot cocoa served and gifts given to children on the good list. Santa stops at each seat to talk to the kids on board and give them their souvenir. The train is decked out with lights and plays Christmas music during your journey. After the ride, you can visit the indoor heated Model Railroad Exhibit and the historic trains in the museum barns.

✓ *How to be a best mom:*

- **Warm up inside of the model train building where you can see a replica of Wisconsin Dells.**
- **Dance in the foam snow near the decorated train exhibit.**

Best Drive-Through Light Show

FESTIVAL OF LIGHTS

Sinnissippi Park
1401 N 2nd St.
4thandlights.com

Stay cozy while experiencing the Christmas spirit at Festival of Lights! This yearly holiday light show is held at Sinnissippi Park from the end of November through New Year's Day. Completely volunteer run, the festival does not charge admission, but community donations keep the lights on year after year.

The Festival of Lights is a drive-through-only event that typically runs Thursdays through Sundays in December with extended hours the week of Christmas and the week after. Beautiful light displays, created and sponsored by local businesses and individuals, are set up on the path around the park. Guests are instructed to tune to a local radio station to listen to Christmas music as they drive through. Each year, new displays are added, spanning more of the park. Several impressive features include a 60-foot light tunnel that cars drive through upon entering the park, animated displays that move, and trees strung with dazzling lights. On most weekend evenings, Santa Claus makes an appearance near the donation booth.

One fun way to incorporate the Festival of Lights into your holiday traditions is to go on Christmas Eve. Bring along hot cocoa and cookies for the ride and go in your pajamas. Please note, there is often a wait to see the displays, and the days before Christmas are the busiest.

WOODWARD CHRISTMAS DISPLAY

5001 N 2nd St., Loves Park | 815-639-6447

Local business Woodward also has a cute, small Christmas drive-through display that can be viewed throughout the holiday season. They open their gates to a half-circle driveway and allow cars to drive through to view the boxed holiday scenes. The displays are enclosed in glass and include some heartwarming holiday scenes as well as several Nativity scenes. There is also a huge lighted Christmas tree in the center of the driveway. Be sure to stay in the car while you enjoy this light display.

How to be a best mom:

- **Visit Woodward Governor before or after visiting the Festival of Lights in Sinnissippi Park for a double dose of Christmas light fun.**
- **If you're heading down 251 (North Second Street), drive through the Trickie's light display on the Frontage Road if their gates are open.**

GOEBBERT'S DRIVE THRU LIGHT SHOW

42W813 Reinking Rd., Pingree Grove | 847-464-5952
goebberts.com

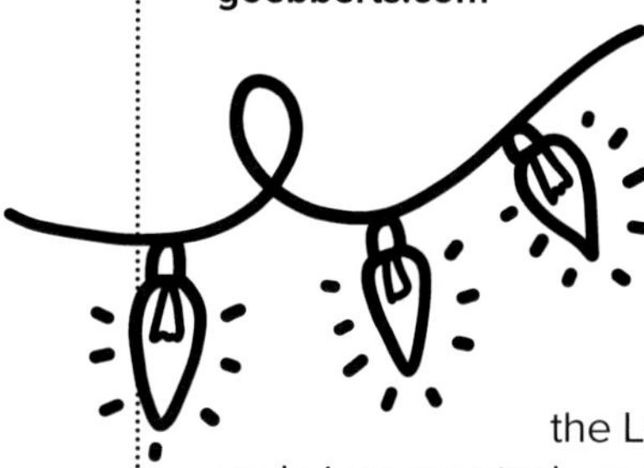

Head to Pingree Grove for an epic drive-through Christmas light experience at Goebbert's. Goebbert's Drive Thru Light Show has two separate experiences available. The first is a 15-minute drive through the farm's apple orchard to see light displays of all colors, which are coordinated to music. The second is the Larsen's Light Show, which is a 30-minute park-and-view event where families stay in the car. The massive light show includes pyrotechnics, lasers, and thousands of lights displayed on a 100-foot-wide house set to music. They also have a drive-through light experience for Halloween for two weeks prior to the holiday.

How to be a best mom:

- **Bring hot cocoa and snacks to enjoy in the car and plan for at least around an hour to wait and see the lights.**
- **During October, pay a visit to the Halloween version of the light show.**

Best Walk-Through Holiday Lights

ALL AGLOW

1354 N 2nd St. | 815-987-8858
nicholasconservatory.com/all-aglow

Bundle up and enjoy the light show at All Aglow! Since 2013, Nicholas Conservatory & Gardens has been decked out with thousands of lights to become a sparkling wonderland for the holidays. The All Aglow display runs from the day after Thanksgiving to early January. Admission is free, and it's open daily from dusk until dawn. This exhibit is walk-through only. It is accessible for both wheelchairs and strollers, though navigation may be difficult during busier times of day.

This outdoor display features light-wrapped trees, shrubs, and stand-alone decorations. The display path follows a one-way loop that starts at the parking lot for Nicholas Conservatory and then winds its way down the sidewalks, around the Eclipse Lagoon, and through the rose garden. From there, families switch over to the Rock River Recreation Path to get back to their parking spots.

There are several rainbow-colored tunnels to walk through and 50 jumbo candy canes, all made by hand. Colorful stars line the lagoon, in more than just traditional Christmas colors; expect to see vibrant purples, gorgeous teals, and bright yellows. The Nicholas Conservatory's lights are directly across the street from the Festival of Lights' drive-through holiday display in Sinnissippi Park. Many people make an evening out of walking through the Nicholas Conservatory grounds and then warming up on a drive through the Festival of Lights.

ILLUMINATED

318 Spring Creek Rd. | 815-229-9390
andersongardens.org

Bundle up and take a stroll through the award-winning Anderson Japanese Gardens as they look like you've never seen them. Throughout the months of November and December, the gardens glow with dramatic purple, blue, and gold up-lighting on the trees and bushes. The pond and waterfalls throughout the Japanese gardens reflect the shining lights back to create a magical atmosphere of holiday cheer. On select nights, families can listen to local school choirs singing carols and enjoy made-to-order wood-fired pizza and hot chocolate from Rockford Roasting Company.

✓ *How to be a best mom:*

- **Grab a hot cocoa from Rockford Roasting Company before you walk around the outdoor lights.**
- **Be sure to dress for the weather, the entire display is outdoors.**

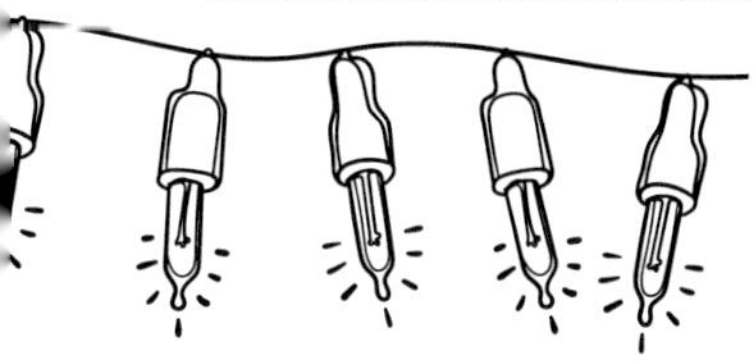

HOLIDAY LIGHT SHOW

1455 Palmer Dr., Janesville WI
rbgholidaylightshow.com

The biggest and brightest walk-through holiday light show is just over the state line in Janesville, Wisconsin. The Holiday Light Show at Rotary Botanical Gardens is an incredible display of over 1.5 million lights including lights strung from trees, walls of lights, and luminaria lighting the path. These lights come in every color imaginable and surround the pathway throughout the gardens. There are plenty of photo opportunities throughout the walk, and the comfort station in the middle of the gardens sells sugar cookies and hot cocoa for a sweet treat to keep you warm. The gardens take between one to two hours to walk through and are worth paying a visit!

✓ *How to be a best mom:*

- **Plan a visit on an evening with snow to see the lights sparkle even more.**
- **Purchase the 3D glasses that make the lights look snowman shaped.**

Best Way to Soar on the Snow

SNOW PARK AT ALPINE HILLS

4402 Larson Ave. | 815-966-8737
alpinehillsadventure.com/snowpark

Shred some snow at Alpine Hills! When the temperature drops and the snow starts flying, Snow Park at Alpine Hills offers tubing and snowboarding. The snow park relies on nature to provide some of the snow, but they also have snowmaking machines that can beef up a stingy snowfall. The snow park's season typically lasts from December through early March.

This is one place where parents can have just as much fun as their kids. Kids over 42 inches tall can ride on their own in a blue tube; those between 36 to 42 inches tall can ride in a red mini tube tethered to an adult. The tubing experience is a fast and fun ride to the bottom of a three-lane hill and then a quick ride back up on a moving walkway. Tubing is the most popular attraction at the park, so reservations are recommended.

Located next to the tubing hill, a terrain park for snowboarders includes boxes and rails to grind on as well as hills to snowboard down. Snowboards and helmets can be rented, or you can bring your own. Equipment must have metal edges; no all-plastic snowboards are allowed. The snow park also offers snowboarding lessons. After a day in the snow, families can head up to the lodge to enjoy some hot cocoa in the heated lobby.

Parents can have just as much fun as their kids!

TWIN SISTERS PARK

3001 Harney Ct.
rockfordparkdistrict.org/sledding

Get your snow pants on, pack the sled in the car, and head to Twin Sisters Park for some serious sledding. Twin Sisters Park is a very popular sledding destination with large, somewhat steep hills. This location can get busy on snowy weekends so you may want to go during the school day with little ones or immediately after school with the whole family. Grab a coffee or hot chocolate from the nearby Velvet Robot and enjoy some time hanging out in their retro shop. There are board games and some video games that you can play for free while you're there!

How to be a best mom:

- **Pack hot cocoa and some snacks to enjoy in the car after you're done sledding.**
- **Go sledding on weekday afternoons or early in the morning to avoid crowds.**

ANNA PAGE PARK

3102 N Springfield Ave. | 815-987-8800
rockfordparkdistrict.org/anna-page-park

Another prime sledding location in Rockford is Anna Page Park. The park was the former home of a 250-foot toboggan chute that was removed in the '90s, but the spot still remains popular for sledding. The park has smaller, gentle hills that are great for younger kids or first-timers. If you work up an appetite after sledding for a few hours, stop by the Olympic Tavern for some lunch in a cozy atmosphere. The Olympic Tavern has been a staple in Rockford for over 75 years and serves American comfort food that all ages will enjoy.

How to be a best mom:

- **Come back to Anna Page Park in the spring, summer, or fall to check out their disc golf course.**
- **Bring an inflatable snow tube to make the sledding experience a little more exciting.**

Best Place for Winter Wonder

ILLINOIS SNOW SCULPTING COMPETITION

1401 N 2nd St. | 815-987-8858
ilsnowsculpting.com

Marvel at intricate sculptures made from ice and snow at Sinnissippi Park! The Illinois Snow Sculpting Competition happens annually in late January or early February at Sinnissippi Park. Since 1987, this competition has brought teams from around the state to face off for the right to represent Illinois in the US National Snow Sculpting Competition.

Sculptors are each given a block of snow, which is six feet long, six feet wide, and 10 feet tall. Nothing except snow, ice, and water may be added to the snow. Sculptors are not allowed to use power tools. The snow sculptures are judged on creativity, technique, and message. The sculptors only have three days to sculpt. Families can visit the park multiple times during the event to see the works in progress or just attend on Saturday afternoon to check out the winners. Aside from the professional competition, there is also a high school division, which pits area high schoolers against each other.

In years past, the sculptures have featured animals like owls and blowfish as well as historical figures like Abraham Lincoln and Pocahontas. Many of the sculptures have immense detail. Admission is free, but donations are welcome. Families can view the snow sculptures from sunrise until 10 p.m. Parking is limited at Sinnissippi Park, but overflow parking is available across the street at Nicholas Conservatory.

ECLIPSE LAGOON

1354 N 2nd St. | 815-987-8858
nicholasconservatory.com/lagoon

When weather permits and the ice is four to six inches thick, Eclipse Lagoon opens for public ice-skating and hockey from 9 a.m. to 10 p.m. daily. The Rockford Park District keeps the lagoon smooth and clean with a resurfacer. Skating is free. Bring your own ice skates or rent a pair from inside the Nicholas Conservatory on select dates and times. Hockey goals are also available to borrow for free on a first-come, first-served basis. Heated restrooms are available in the outdoor pavilion. The Lagoon has lights so people can safely skate after nightfall.

✓ *How to be a best mom:*

- **Make a yearly tradition out of ice skating on the Lagoon with your family.**
- **Visit between November and early January to skate surrounded by holiday lights.**

ATWOOD PARK

2685 New Milford Rd. | 815-966-8747
atwoodpark.org

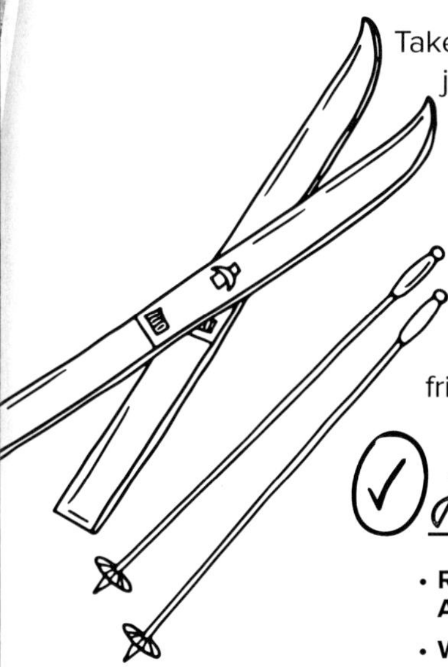

Take the kids to try snowshoeing, cross-country skiing, or just go for a winter hike, at Atwood Park. Atwood Park rents cross-country skis, snowshoes, and even mountain bikes for winter fun on the trails. Atwood Park spans more than 334 acres that includes forest, marsh, and prairieland. There are five miles of multiuse trails within the park for hikers, bikers, and cross-county skiers. Don't forget to stop by the unique Birds of Prey exhibit to see the feathered friends enjoying the snow!

✓ *How to be a best mom:*

- **Rent cross-country skis or snowshoes from Rocktown Adventures before you go.**
- **Warm up in the lodge and check out the reptiles that call it home.**

Index

Loves Park

Cherry Valley

Roscoe

Rockton

Belvidere